UFOs

The Truth You'll Wish You Didn't Know.

Ray Russell

UFOs: The Truth You'll Wish You Didn't Know

ISBN: 978-0-9840821-9-3
R.R. Bowker, LLC
Chatham, New Jersey

Thinking People's Press
Las Vegas, Nevada

Ozymandias
by P.B. Shelley

I met a traveller from an antique land,
Who said: "Two vast and trunkless legs of stone
Stand in the desert. . . Near them, on the sand,
Half sunk a shattered visage lies, whose frown,
And wrinkled lip, and sneer of cold command,
Tell that its sculptor well those passions read.
Which yet survive, stamped on these lifeless things,
The hand that mocked them, and the heart that fed;
And on the pedestal, these words appear:
'My name is Ozymandias, King of Kings;
Look on my Works, ye Mighty, and despair!'
Nothing beside remains. Round the decay
Of that colossal wreck, boundless and bare,
The lone and level sands stretch far away."

Prologue

What really happened at Roswell in 1947?
Was there a coverup?
Are alien abductions real?
Why are there so many UFO sightings at military bases?
What's behind recent revelations about UFOs and UAPs?
Why are there so many more sightings nowadays?

Herein lay some *real* answers.
Unless you are psychotic, you are *not* going to like them.

I tell you now that the UFO/UAP phenomena are real. I will use "UAP" in the literal sense: stuff in the sky that we are unable to identify. I will use "UFO" in the sense of these objects being craft piloted by intelligent biological entities that are from elsewhere. I shall refer to these beings simply as "Kalltus," "Them," and "They" (capital) throughout this book, with an explanation as to why included. I cannot tell you definitively whether or not they are people of earth from another time, but they *almost* certainly are not. I will tell you what these beings have to say about time travel later. I will also say that they are not *from* another dimension (see Afterword), and that the notion of being from a 'parallel dimension' is merely a manifestation of humanity's childlike ignorance. More on these matters later.

Please stop reading now if you are one of those people who believes that every time you see something new that seems to conflict with something that you *think* you know, the new information is wrong; clinging to baseless beliefs and being unable to integrate painful, factual truths into our thinking is one of the major factors in our undoing, according to Them. Reading further would thus be pointless for those with closed or narrow minds. I am emphatically ***not*** saying that you should not be critical in your thinking. On the contrary, I am saying the opposite. However, there is a difference between thinking critically and thinking that something must be incorrect just because you cannot understand it, it defies what you think that you already know or that it conflicts with your belief system. Einstein fell into that trap (*see* page 102). Park your Dunning-Kruger and be better than Einstein.

This is the truth.
It sucks.
It's going to hurt.

Any time that I have intentionally changed some name or factual detail (I did it quite a bit), it will be for the sole purpose of avoiding giving internet trolls any clues for hunting down the still-living people involved. The fact that the chronology is very *Pulp Fiction* is for the same reason: the people who know this stuff, to an individual, want no part of this story being revealed. In fact, anybody who already knows what is about to be told will be mortified and incensed that I am telling you the truth. Should you come across what you believe to be some sort of a continuity error, paradox, contradiction or otherwise, I assure you that it is deliberately so, and for the same reason.

I suggest that you focus on the underlying message.

I began writing this around 2004, so I have had a fair amount of time to get it just so. I apologize to those who are distracted by such matters, those who may ultimately miss the point of the entire book because you live to find fault in details. That's on you, and that is, again, part of the problem. You probably ought to consider ceasing to be such a smarmy, pedantic tosser. Your friends (assuming that you have any), colleagues and family will appreciate it very much. Thank you.

You will soon be made aware of why I went to such lengths to protect the memories of the brave and tortured men and women who carry this knowledge.

For everyone else, I endeavor to tell you as accurately as a man who is trying to stay two steps ahead of the Reaper can recall, everything that I was told in the hopes that They were incorrect and that you will do something about it; not for my sake, but for your own.

I initially set out to write this in the third person: a character named Hermes discovered his father's secret journals... In the end, it just felt too contrived, as if I was trying to write a screenplay to sell. If someone else wants to turn this into a movie, I will gladly consent. Anything that spreads the word will help our situation. My own father urged me to just tell it straight. After lengthy consideration, I believe that this is the proper course of action. I apologize to those who had their hearts set upon a wild yarn with car chases, evil secret agents and gunplay.

Contained herein are the recollections of conversations I had with my father. He was very smart. He was very well connected. He was also in a perfect position to know the truth. In his later years, he began telling me all of the things contained herein. I simply do as he asked: sound the alarm, tell the world what he knew, try to get people to see what must be done. He believed that whether or not you accept where he received the information from, it is not incorrect. It is in fact one hundred percent accurate.

It is painful.
It is frightening.
It is absolutely true.

All that you have to do is keep an open mind and *think*. Think for yourself. Do not let others think for you, especially if the others are "UFO researchers," debunkers (*Klassholes*, explained later), priests, politicians or academics, none of who are any better than the average human at keeping their ignorance and egos in check. In the final analysis, you should come to realize that the lack of open minds and critical thinking are at the heart of what ultimately shall haunt the memory of our planet.

One of the last things that my father said to me was in response to these questions:

"What if everyone misses the point, getting caught up in trying to determine who you and I are, or just arbitrarily reject this information because they think that they are smarter and better informed than they really are? What if nobody heeds this?"

His response was swift and certain.

"Then we will all perish."

R.R, 2024

This page was intentionally left blank.

1

"They" Are Real

My father was in the intelligence game. That's how he referred to it. He and my mother adopted me during World War II when I was six, a gift that I am eternally grateful for. Dad, the ink on his sheepskin still crisp, bounced around the globe during the war, as much of the information to which he was privy was deemed to be too sensitive for electronic transmission. His primary job during the War was to make sure that certain communications between high level figures got to and from point to point securely. His secondary job, the more complicated one, was a natural consequence of the first. If a person has valuable secrets, others will try to get their mitts on them. Never letting his guard down, he was constantly noting every person paying him attention, gathering as much information as he could about them, and figuring out who they worked for. He kept it all in his head even after filing official reports. Over fifty years after the war, he regaled me with names, dates and locations of so many pivotal events of World War II, the Korean War and the Vietnam War.[1] His mind and his memory were things of beauty, enviable by any standard. My own work tests the bounds of what the human mind is capable of, yet compared to Dad, I always felt like I belonged on the little bus.

He was exceptionally good at his job, dodging honey traps, abduction attempts, drugging, and on at least two occasions, assassination. He was also a vault: to my knowledge, I am the only unauthorized person to whom he has ever given any classified information, and even then it was for the sole purpose of me telling this story after he died. By the end of the war he was considered to be about as solid and capable an intel officer as any nation could ever hope for. It was for those reasons that he was brought into the "dark side" of the government.

I can say with great certainty that Dad was not cut out for field work. By *field work*, I mean actual spying and intelligence gathering. I have no knowledge of him ever doing any nor ever even being asked to do it. He was an unassuming man of smallish stature. His back had been severely injured in a train crash when he was a teen, so he moved gingerly, though not obviously so, had difficulty climbing multiple flights of stairs, and was incapable of carrying even a courier bag weighing more than ten kilos for very long without debilitating discomfort setting in. As it

---

[1] Dad said: "Vietnam and Korea were wars. If anyone says that they weren't, if they call them 'conflicts,' they are either a lying twat or a goddamned idiot. Any time a million and a half corpses litter the landscape, it's a bloody war."

happened, his injury was a blessing, because it kept him out of the shooting war and got him into intelligence.

His natural gifts were in mathematics, science and in reading people, all of which made him exceptional at his job in so many ways. True analytical prowess and keen intuition (he called it, "non-verbal listening skills") made him excellent at sniffing out most B.S. and danger, particularly from Westerners, and most especially from high level American leadership types, both military and political. Hyper-observant and constantly vigilant, he was most formidable.

Rather than going into the Signal Security Corps and Comint, he went to the OSS and then to the CIA after the war. The National Security Act threw the intelligence gathering arm of the government into the same bed with the part that plotted action based on that intelligence. He was there early on and saw just how unwise such an *all eggs in one basket* approach to intelligence is. But that was how he was in a position to learn what he learned. When there were *real* secrets in play, you wanted and needed people with his repertoire, experience, commitment to mission and tight lips. Not everyone was so noble nor so smart.

It was in late 1947, just after that consolidation of power into the CIA, that Dad became aware of what people popularly call, "The Roswell Incident." It infuriated him to no end that the chuckleheads in the military had screwed that situation up so badly.

The United States did *not* want, "the bloody Reds" to get any clues as to how we were monitoring them (especially when it came to the atomic bomb). Roswell could have given them a big hint on that account. But trying to cover up a, "We have a secret way of remotely monitoring your atomic bomb tests" truth with a, "We captured spacemen driving a Hewson Rocket" lie had the opposite effect, at least initially.

It all came about because a few ordinary citizens got it into their heads that some crash debris that was located in the middle of the high desert had to be an alien spacecraft. There was metallic stuff. There was high-tech looking stuff. UFO fever was rampant at the time, as was paranoia about the Russians, so every light in the post-war sky was imagined to be little green men, possibly working with the Russkies. When the military authorities dispatched to investigate the debris field arrived at the scene, they were confronted with things that most of them had never seen before. The power of suggestion being what it is, those men *heard* aliens and so "*saw*" what they expected. At least some of them did. The ones who knew that a classified high altitude ballon (they did not know what it was for) was MIA suffered no such misconception. But someone leaked the crashed saucer story and the scoop-happy press ran with it. Then the military *idiotically confirmed* the crashed saucer story, believing that it would be a perfect cover for the truth. They did not anticipate that what it really would do is draw way more attention than they wanted.

According to Dad, the secret program that lost the balloon was such a big deal that FBI special agents were sent into Roswell to listen in on all of the local scuttlebutt and report back the swirling rumors. A few agents were also dispatched to interview witnesses in order to make sure that they didn't know anything important and then to swear them to secrecy regardless of what they said. Bear in mind that *none* of those agents knew what had really happened. The agents simply recorded what people were saying and passed it up the chain of command so that the "top people" could determine its value. Most of the FBI agents were smart enough to know that it was not a crashed weather balloon; why in the hell would Uncle Sam send a team to the middle of literally nowhere for that? So if a witness said that they saw space aliens with ray guns eating armadillos, the agents swore them to secrecy upon pain of pain or worse. It's easy to see how such citizens thought that the government was suppressing "the truth".

As one might imagine, Uncle Sam was not pulling senior agents off of their pressing work to go eat barbecue with a bunch of yokels in Podunk, New Mexico. Mostly junior agents were sent. These young go-getters, several of them on their rookie-season assignments in the field, got all gussied up in their Sunday best to impress and intimidate the rubes; hence the 'men in black' stories. It was just a bunch of overly enthusiastic youngsters playing big shot.

The military brass, as one might naturally expect, pooped their panties when they realized that the crashed disk story was going global with ridiculous speed. At the time, they had reason to believe that there was a good chance that the Russians knew about what was going on in the New Mexico outback. There had already been some high value chatter that there had been spies in the Manhattan Project, leaking secrets to friends and enemies alike. Hence the hastily arranged, highly awkward press conference to kill the crashed UFO story, featuring some faked up shredded weather balloon corpse and the red-faced, contrite looking Major Jesse Marcel.

Early on, a few people involved at Roswell did indeed believe the UFO lie; many military personnel bought into it hook, line and sinker. But the "reverse cover story" (weather balloons) quelled the public interest quickly. That pre-Francis Gary Powers generation would drink the government's pruno and cheerfully pretend that it was cabernet, no questions asked. It was only decades later, when the ex-military "crashed UFO believers" started to reach their expiration dates that they began telling their heartfelt, factually false stories to anyone who would listen.

What made matters far worse was that Maj. Marcel had taken pieces of the actual non-weather balloon wreckage from the crash site home to his ten-year old son and told the boy that it was crashed UFO debris. That kid, seeing strange things for the first and only time in his life, believed his dad. He grew up believing his dad, reinforcing the story in his mind's eye. Then tiny Marcel grew up to become a doctor. Dr. Marcel told his story of handling UFO debris with conviction and sophistication, which makes sense given how it all came about. His credibility was rarely questioned because he was a doctor. That is sheer stupidity because: (1) doctors are just people, replete with observational errors, psychological issues (confabulation, suggestion etc.) (2) some doctors are truly idiots, and most importantly (3) Dr. Marcel wasn't a bloody doctor when he saw top secret nuclear monitoring equipment as a ten year old! He was a child who believed what Major Daddy had told him: *crashed UFO*. Then he spent a lifetime burning that belief into his cerebellum.

My Dad was always mystified as to how some of these people confabulated the facts, or worse, imagined or made up details that never existed. But in the end, one thing was clear. There were no aliens at Roswell. There were no spaceships. There were no crashes. There were no conversations with captured aliens and there were no alien autopsies. As a matter of fact, as far as he knew, (and he would have been someone who would have known) no crashed alien disc was ever recovered on U.S. soil *nor anywhere else*.

Throughout the 1950s, 60s and 70s, he heard a lot of scuttlebutt about foreign countries having recovered crashed discs, particularly in Central America and South America, but none of those wild tales ever amounted to anything other than hot gas. As he put it to me much later, "Klaatus[2] can travel a trillion-trillion kilometers without hitting a speck of space dust and then bullseye Malmstrom AFB in a pea soup fog. If you're so daft that you believe that They are running out of gas, smashing into jets, unable to survive a lightning strike, can get taken down by one of our primitive missiles or that They are just crashing willy-nilly like Mr. Magoo, I've got a bridge in Brooklyn that I'd love to sell you for just a small down payment. *They* are *never*

---

[2] "Klaatu" was the name Dad and his colleagues used for Them. It came from the name of the alien in the movie, *The Day the Earth Stood Still*. You should have known that.

crashing." There was a pregnant pause that I finally breached.

"So it's all just a load of B.S.?" I asked.

"CHRIST, NO! They're as real you and I. They're just unimaginably technologically ahead of us and They are superior aviators."

That was the moment, in the late 1980's, that I became very conflicted. A lifetime of knowing that he was privy to juicy information that *nobody* outside of his top tier government circle were ever supposed to know and that he had sworn an oath to keep secret, ran headlong into my opinion that much of what he possibly knew was too valuable and important to be held by a cabal of what I perceived to be dark forces within the government, hell bent on exploiting the information for personal, political and military power.

Dad was also getting older, and if Grandpa was any sort of indicator, Dad was possibly going to become forgetful and start to mentally unravel over the next decade or so. On top of all of that was one fact about my father that had been bothering me for some time: he was a life-long conservative, red blooded *American government appartchik.* Yet sometime in the early 1980's he abruptly got soft: he started recycling and composting, started riding a bicycle rather than driving most of the time, installed solar panels, joined World Against War, read about the environment... he was listing heavily to port. The day he said that Al Gore was right about the environment was the day that I thought he had lost his mind. Abrupt changes like that in people over forty portend something, and it usually isn't good.

Setting aside my discomfort, I started feeling him out.

This was no easy task. It is important to remember that father was old school; he was of the mind that the government protects The People. The men and women entrusted with safeguarding the nation's secrets swore an oath for a purpose; whether or not to share information was above their pay grade. He was also highly trained and massively experienced. I was not going to be the first person to try to illicit information out of him. The advantages that I had were that I was family, he respected my intellect and he was no less aware of his impending and inevitable meeting with the grim reaper than I was. I decided that my first course of action was to get him to question the logic and the wisdom of his world view *without once* mentioning the UFOs or Them again.

So I started by mentioning Richard Nixon.

"I've sent smarter and better down the crapper," was his first response. I had known that he was not a Nixon fan, but now I was getting a better feel for the depth of his disdain.

"You taught me that no matter who is elected president, they are *my* president and that I need to support them because to do otherwise would be undermining America," I replied.

"He is an ex-president, not *the* president, so piss on him. He was a statistician."

"Statistician?" I asked.

"You've never heard that, '*There are lies, damned lies, and then there are statistics*?' Why did I pay to send you to college?" That was his go-to line every time he told me something I had either forgotten or did not know, but that he thought that I ought to.

"Mark Twain," I responded.

"I'll award you partial credit. Twain cribbed it off of someone else, didn't know who he stole it from, then he attributed it to the wrong guy later. At least he acknowledged that it wasn't an original thought of his own."

"So what if Nixon was a liar? Show me a leader who doesn't lie and I'll show you an ex-leader. From Benjamin Franklin to Joseph Stalin to Ronald Regan, they all lied. Hell, Churchill said that the truth should *always* be attended by a bodyguard of lies." I knew that would gall him.

"First of all, you smart ass, Churchill said that about *wartime*. He didn't mean it about every waking moment of every bloody day. Nixon was a pathological liar, all day, every day. He and Kissinger both. Second, Churchill lied about a lot of non-wartime matters that he didn't have to, that buoyant hypocrite, but never anything public-sphere important. Third, Nixon saw Eisenhower survive that U2 fiasco and decided that telling the truth was always merely an option and never a default. Dumb bastard never even thought to consider the consequences."[3]

"Consequences?" I asked. "What consequences?" He gave me a long, piercing stare before responding.

"You're old enough to know that not all lies are created equally. Telling the people of America that the economy will be fine when you *know* that we are in for a bumpy ride can instill confidence in people and possibly smooth out some of the jolts, a little or a lot. But engaging in wholesale criminal activity and then lying your ass off in order to save your own damned skin, that's just selfish. I'm not talking about Watergate. That was just the KS lesion that tipped the public off to what we in the government already knew: Nixon was AIDS incarnate.[4] I'm talking about the illegal bombing raids in southeast Asia, the civilian death toll, the crimes committed by soldiers on his direct orders ... those lies were to save his *own fucking face* and to avoid *personal* responsibility."

I'd not heard Dad drop an f-bomb in decades, as he had always been a right and proper gentleman in all of his acts and mannerisms. He was riled up and on a roll.

---

[3] President Dwight Eisenhower looked directly into the television camera and flat out lied to the American people from the Oval Office for the first time. He said that the Russians did not shoot down an American U2 spy plane over Russia, which they actually had.

[4] Kaposi sarcoma, a kind of cancer, shows up visually as red or purple lesions on the skin. People with AIDS get them far more frequently than the public generally. The presence of such a KS lesion leads doctors to check for HIV and cancer asap.

"So, the consequences, you ask? He made this country look like a bunch of two-faced arseholes to the rest of the world. It led others to believe that his toxic personality sociopathy was the way of things in American government. It gave rise to unAmerican psychopaths like Lee Atwater, Roger Stone and Paul Manafort who all suckled at the teat of that bleeding rat bastard Roy Cohn, who was satan incarnate. We used to call Stone, Manafort and Atwater *the Unholy Trinity* because they made Tricky Dicky look like Ghandi. But the worst part of it? The American people became as cynical and nihilistic as those mingers. We the People lost our faith in our government. *We* believe nothing. Nixon set us on this path where any time the government does something illegal or unAmerican, they and their supporters can start a bloody conspiracy theory that always gets traction with a large swath of the people. That allows them to avoid the full consequences of their misdeeds. Nixon and the Unholy Trinity sodomized the American spirit. No lube. It was only fitting that Atwater died of ass cancer, but even that was too good for the sod. You can mark my words, their radioactive legacy is far from over."[5]

I suspected that he thought that I was working him by pushing such a hot button. The funny thing was that after a few weeks of such back and forths, I could tell that he had things in his personal vault that he had *wanted* to tell

---

[5] That conversation took place long before the political rise of Donald "Dunning-Kruger" Trump who was also, not coincidentally, an acolyte and mega-fanboy of Roy Cohn.

someone for a while. It wasn't one of those "I've got a secret that I'm just bursting to tell" kind of thing. It was more like when a murderer is racked by so much guilt that they just need to get it off of their chest, confessional kind of a thing. I needed to be patient and wait for him to decide that it was the right time to purge.

So now I had the ball rolling. I kept having regular conversations with him about the Korean war, Vietnam, Lockheed, Boeing, nuclear weapons, Iran-Contra, space weapons... everything *but* Them, Their vehicles... and Area 51.

That was something else that I knew a thing or three about. I had asked him a question about Area 51 once and was sternly told to, "*never* mention that again." At least he did me the courtesy of not denying its existence. I was playing the long game, yet always exercising extreme caution, so I steered clear out of prudence.

Over the following years I learned a lot. Not just about Them, but about so many things that would make most non-insane Americans livid if they knew about them; for example, there was a secret assassination program that targeted Americans. It was based on some post-Nixon era government type's admiration of the Israeli's ability to take out known enemies and *suspected* enemies.

America had gotten up to some seriously shady shit since 1947. But as much as all of that fascinated me, I was starting to wonder if Dad was ever going to tell me about aliens and UFOs.

And then along came the man who shook it all loose,

Bob Lazar.

2

Bob and Janet

Robert Lazar appeared to be an enigma and I was aiming to exploit that. In the early 1990's I asked my dad for his thoughts on Lazar. I shan't bore any of the UFO "aficionados" out there with the details of Bob. Suffice it to say, B.S. Lazar (that's really his name) claimed to be a physicist who had worked at Area 51 on reverse-engineering alien technology from crashed UFOs. For a while, he was *the* catalyst for and the poster child of, the modern UFO movement. He was also the impetus for every UFO fruit loop to re-energize their flagging batteries; those people who "want to believe" so badly that they are willing to overlook the Alaska-sized gaping holes in Bob's ever evolving tale were becoming more vocal and certain of the righteousness and correctness of their causes. Let's put it this way: if there had not been a Bob Lazar, there would have been no X-Files.

"Do you think that this guy's full of beans?" I asked Dad one day.

"Anyone who knows anything for real... you'll never hear their names or see their faces. If we even think about talking to a reporter, we're dead before our next breath."

"So he's just a flimflam man?"

"Yes, but he's probably someone who worked in the business at a really low level... like a maintenance man, equipment manager or janitor in New Mexico. Perhaps he has read some pop-science stuff so he can sling the lingo to the red-meat believers and pass himself off as a scientist. It's simple if you think about it. All he had to do was keep his head down and listen. Many of those Los Alamos scientists rotate in and out of Groom (Area 51) or work in concert with them. Do you get what I mean? Mopping the floor in a dining hall at Los Alamos, a person can overhear more than enough passing conversation to sound like an insider. But just because there are raisins in there, that doesn't make it a spotted dick."[6]

"To what end, though? I mean, why would someone risk the ridicule? Why would he claim to be something that others can easily prove to be a lie?" I asked.

"Oh I can think of a couple of reasons." He said smugly. "Have *you* ever been famous? I'm not talking Schwarzenegger famous here, just sort-of famous. He's like a rock star in the nutter circles. And have you seen him? I'll bet that before he got famous, his only girlfriends were Thumbolina and the Phalanges. On top of that, you can make a boatload of money selling books, doing lecture

---

[6] Spotted dick is a bread pudding that has raisins in it. "Dick" is an old Gaelic word for dough, and the raisins are the spotted part.

circuits, selling tee shirts... It's way too enticing a proposition for most people to resist."

"Well then why is there a disinformation campaign against him?" I clapped back.

"No idea." He replied, nonplussed. "We aren't doing it though. When we do it, you know it. It's scorched earth; total and brutal and ruthless. In the eventuality that we don't kill you before you can leak, we'll make you bloody well wish that we had."

I was ready for that. "The government *officially* denies that he ever even worked for them. How does that reconcile with what you said?" That made him hot. He *loathed* being called out by people who are wrong.

"Why did I shell out good money for you to go to college? Think about it! Here's how that played out. A news reporter called up some primate at the General Services Administration and asked whether Robert Lazar was ever a physicist at Los Alamos. The clerk pokes that query into a computer and says that there was no scientist, physicist or otherwise, on record named Robert Lazar. What the government never denied was that he was ever a janitor, equipment calibrator, maintenance man, food service provider or what have you. They also didn't deny that Lazar may have been a flunky with one of the contractors that had minimal access to non-secured areas. He may be able to show that he *was* at some facility but he sure as hell can't prove that he was a physicist at Groom, Los Alamos, Oak Ridge, Tatooine or anywhere else, because he wasn't. I'd bet he's never even *seen* Groom because if he had been there, he'd know that there are no aliens or alien space craft. The boy has just enough truthful information to weave a sellable yarn, that's all."

"Then how does he know about Janet?" I asked. Janet, also known as The Red Stripe, is the jet (there are more than one of them) that ferries the workers into and out of Area 51 who aren't enamored with the alternative: a long ride on a crappy bus across a scorching desert. That seemed to really rile him up.

"Who *doesn't* know about Janet? It's not a bloody state secret! You can see the blasted thing leaving as bold as brass from the Las Vegas airport in broad daylight every day, as regular as Canada geese! That's a staple of the lore of those tossers. I'm sure that he went to some UFO convention or read one of those paranormal magazines that their types publish and picked that up."

I backed off, but after a few minutes he launched back into it.

"If this knob head wants to keep pushing it, he'll scrounge up a few more interesting tidbits of truth to bolster his tosh. But he will never have a smoking gun, because there isn't one. Groom and the test site are the worst kept secrets on earth. Hell, the Reds knew about it way back when we started doing skunk work. If you knew the things that we did to screw with the Russians back then, you'd bust a bloody stitch! They all knew, including China. Why do you think the nutters changed their story? Crashed disks at Groom Lake. Crashed disks in 'Hangar 18' on Wright-Patterson. Alien bodies in Brazil. Underground bunkers in the arctic... Every time their stories start unraveling in the face of actual facts, they just weave up a new fable."

I got a couple of beers for us out of the refrigerator, wishing that he had something stronger in the house because I was going to shoot for the moon. It turns out that my worries were unwarranted. As we sat there drinking and listening to Benny Goodman, Dad turned toward me.

"The truth is," his face was stony, eyes like glass, "Klaatu... the one who contacted us... it seems to me that he's trying to help us."

3

What Else is Real

"What do you mean?" The words came out of my mouth in an instant.

"They are not supposed to contact us. It almost seemed like Klaatu knew that he was breaking the rules." My mind raced and spun simultaneously as I listened.

"Klaatu, as in a single individual alien? Contacted us? How? When?"

He sat there frozen, staring at me almost as if his brain was overwhelmed by what he was contemplating revealing. Finally he said, "He did. He came to us...the good guys...Westerners."

"Do you mean that he didn't contact the Russians or Chinese?" I asked.

"As far as I know, Klaatu just talked to us and the Brits. But I don't think that he was supposed to. At least not to the extent that he did."

My heart was in my throat and it was roaring like an F1 race car on the *autobahn*. I had this ONE piece of information and I could feel my brain overheating, literally. My head was hot and beads of sweat were forming on my superorbital ridge. I took a swig of beer to try to cool off. It did not improve my condition. I could not fathom how Dad's head hadn't completely melted years ago. I leaned closer to him and I put my hand on his arm. "Do you want to tell me about it?" Dad took a deep breath.

"It was England. That's where it started. People all over the world had been seeing the craft for eons. But they were always just superficial sightings, and mostly by civilians with no frame of reference for anything like size or speed. But that time in England, that was deliberate. One of Them was trying to 'out' Themselves. That much seemed pretty obvious."

"Was that at Bentwaters?" I whispered. His face finally betrayed subtle emotion; one corner of his mouth twitched just a hair, hinting at a Harrison Ford, Indiana Jones grin.

"Yes. It was 1959. That was the trip over that I *had* to take. Your mother was hacked off at me for going because it was on our anniversary, but I'm damned glad that I went. The Brits had been chasing radar ghosts and visual sightings for years all around there. We knew it wasn't chicanery (meaning that it was not a secret project by another government agency spoofing RADAR signals) so our military leaders were all quite shaken by the prospect that the Ivans had finally squeezed their Jerries (former Nazi scientists) for something interesting and were using it to run recon on the UK... or worse. But it was on that trip, 1959, when we figured out that it wasn't the Reds and it wasn't from earth."

"How? H.. how did you know?" I stammered.

"The Brits had a pretty laissez faire attitude about such things. They were basically in denial, self-convinced that it was a foreign power probing them and their air-defense perimeter. They would scrambled jets with regularity, even when they knew that they didn't have to. If any of the targets were Russian, so their thinking went, scrambling fighters to chase targets that were known to be imaginary would give the Reds the impression that we are easily fooled. Misinformation is nearly as valuable as information.

"One night, one of the Brit's intel chaps, we called him 'Spooner,' failed to show up for his shift.[7] He had taken a walk, leaving his post without permission, and turned up the next morning with superficial burns on the left side of his face. Obviously his commanding officer wanted a *whiskey tango foxtrot* chat with him ASAP. Spooner told him that he had heard a voice inside of his head that told him where to go in the woods, but that the voice didn't say *why* he was supposed to go."

"You must go to the Dagobah system." I said like Sir Alec Guinness.

"Exactly so. Spooner said that when he got into the woods, there was a round, disk-like craft that was hovering about a meter off of the ground. It was roughly eight meters in diameter and that there was a glow between the disk and the ground that looked incorrect to him, as if it was a bad

---

[7] "Spooner" was a reference to a character that appeared on a breakfast cereal box from that era named "Spoon-sized." The intelligence man was rather diminutive. The characters on the box were spacemen of some sort, at least that is how Dad recalled it being. Anyway, they free-associated in the moment.

artist's rendition of what it should look like. He said that it was as if light shined up from the ground to illuminate the underside of the disk, and down onto the ground to illuminate the soil, but that the light was coming from neither above nor below. It was as if a bubble of light hovered between the disk and the ground like a cushion."

"Daaaaaamn," I said in a long, drawn out exhale. "It floated on an energy bubble! Did it leave any physical evidence behind?"

"Nothing. No impressions in the dirt, no radiation... not a bleeding lepton. But that was the least interesting part. Spooner said that there was a Klattu just standing there next to the craft. The Klaatu didn't speak, but it was like They were putting thoughts into his head. I'll get to why I say 'They' in a bit. Spooner was really rattled by that; he wasn't hearing voices, and there were no sentences. It was as if entire ideas just appeared inside of his head in a flash. He suddenly knew things and believed them to be absolutely true." Dad leaned back into his chair and took a drink, adjusting his back with a pillow. He had a look of relief mingled with fear.

"The first idea he received," Dad continued between swigs of beer, "was that the Klaatus were not here for any malicious purpose. They were *all* here simply to survey the planet. It was not for the purpose of conquest. They had no interest in our weapons nor in our defensive capabilities because earth life was so far behind them in every way that we literally posed zero threat to them. They made it clear that this included our 'primitive' nuclear weapons." He finished his beer and asked for another. I obliged.

"The second thought given to him was that there are many different entities from many different places visiting earth, all for the same purposes and with the same advantages over us." He sat there, staring at the blank, black picture tube of his Sony television for a long moment, as if piecing together what he wanted to say next.

"The third idea that popped into his head was that Spooner was supposed to deliver a message. He wasn't told who to deliver it to, just that he needed to deliver a message. I surmised that they chose him because he was in intel and he was an officer, giving his story more traction with the higher ups. That was important to them, methinks. The message was that They would be making more visits and that They do not want anyone to be frightened by Them. Spooner said that we are supposed to ignore Them, as if They are just another natural phenomena in the world, like bugs or birds. We should not waste any time trying to contact Them, catch Them, study Them nor stop Them. They will never harm us, but we will *never* catch Them nor be remotely capable of impeding Their visits."

I was breathless. I could feel sweat trickling down the back of my neck even though the air conditioning in the older man's home was pegged at sixty-eight degrees. My brain was swimming in what I had just heard, or more accurately, drowning in it.

"What the hell." I finally blurted out. My hand shook as I took another drink. "Was that it? Did he say that anything else happened?"

"The way he described it... It was like all of this happened in a flash, as if zero time elapsed. He said that he 'knew' that They were in his head, as if They had merged themselves with him, and that They answered questions before he realized that he was thinking them; They weren't just reading his mind, They were *part of it* and knew everything in his brain; every memory, every thought, every question." Dad turned to face me. "Have you ever had a dream where something is happening in the dream, like maybe there is a knock at the door, and then you wake up and there really is a knock at your door? Spooner said it was like that. They were answering questions and *then* he thought of the question an instant later. Klaatu *knew* that he and we were worried about Them being aggressors, that we were petrified of the Russians getting their nasty mitts on alien technology... everything."

"Did this Spooner guy remember any of the details of it?" I asked hopefully.

"Oh yes, he did. He claimed to remember everything... more than he could wrap is head around and articulate." Dad seemed to drift in thought, tapering into silence.

"Are you going to tell me or am I going to stroke out and die over here?"

He gave a little laugh that made his head recoil. "Spooner said that he felt like he was in a big room that was really formal, like a library or a courthouse or some such place. He knew that he was standing in the forest and he could see the ship and the Klaatu, but at the same time, he was in a formal meeting environment with carpeted floors and hardwood paneling all about. He wanted to look around but he couldn't turn his head nor his eyes. He said that it *felt* like he was one with the Klaatu, that Their minds were one, but that he could not search his environment. Klaatu had full access to him, but Spooner only got what he was given. He said that he could *feel* Klaatu looking at every part of his mind at once. It made him feel afraid at first, and then violated, but that quickly changed to calm acceptance. I guess Klaatu either mellowed him out or his brain put together that if someone actually knows *every last detail* of what's going on in your brain, there are no secrets, so you might as well surrender to the moment. It's like being naked in church, only exponentially worse, I'd imagine.

"He was trying to figure Them out, good officer that he was, trying to find out what motivates Them, but as I said, he got nothing from Them other than what They wanted to share, which was nil. He said that it was the feeling of a total lack of control, the realization that he was absolutely and completely *owned* by this character that threw him into despair. But Klaatu fixed that too. He told Spooner that They can do this to nearly every person on earth, all at the same time if They so desired. That They haven't, and never will, should comfort him."

"*Nearly*? Did anyone other than me catch that?" I asked, puzzled.

"Yes, They can control *nearly* everyone. I'll get to that another time." Dad said with a sigh.

"How soon after this reported encounter did you talk to him?" I asked. Dad seemed impressed that I didn't accept it as an actual event, merely a reported one.

"It took almost thirty hours for me to get there. Spooner had been interviewed for a few hours immediately after the event by his C.O, base commander and British intelligence. The Brits took blood and hair samples to test for drugs and radiation exposure because more than one of their officers thought Spooner might be on something, or that he was fabricating the whole thing after monkeying around with something hot (radioactive) in order to cover his arse, like he had taken some bird to see a bomb in order to get into her nickers or some such rot.

"By the time I got to him, Spooner had slept for about 18 hours, so he was fairly well rested and much more composed. I had listened to the earlier interview on audio tape before we started in on him. He sounded fairly coherent on the tapes for a guy who had just been brain buggered by E.T, but he did sound exhausted. I spent time at the beginning of my debriefing just trying to figure out whether or not the whole thing was a delusion or a hallucination. I had the company shrink there with me, watching the whole time. Spooner's psych evals up to that point had been spotless and his service record was exemplary. Nothing strange nor stressful afoot in his life either." Dad drew a deep breath. "The Reader's Digest version of it was that he was as sober as a judge and as sane as ..." He struggled for a metaphor. "Everyone's a lunatic, I guess." Dad finished his half-thought.

It seemed to me that Dad was finding his groove now, as though he had slid into what he did best; giving a report to a colleague. I opted to hold my questions and just let him go with the flow.

"The Brits," he continued, "wanted to get him on the box (polygraph) but I advised that they wait until after we had gotten everything that we could out of him, that way they would be able to test him on any details that we deemed critical. But I could tell throughout the interview that Spooner *believed* everything that he was saying was the truth, and that's the only thing that those damned lie detectors tell you. Not to toot my own horn, but I'm better than the bloody box. Too many people in my line of work got a little too comfortable with that machine. They see the damned thing as a CYA measure and as an excuse to not exercise due diligence, as if there is some shortcut to doing legwork. Look at all of the moles in the government who have managed to pass their poly. It's laughable.

"Anyway, Spooner was an intel guy. He wanted information and Klaatu was having none of it. But They told him that They were sorry, that They could not explain the things that he wanted to know because doing so would violate Their rules or principles.

"That was another funny thing. Spooner described Them as having rules and principles, but the concept of laws, written codes that carried sanctions, never entered the picture. It was as if They had gentlemen's handshake agreements and that was that. All of the Klaatus honor the rules, because not following them would lead to anarchy.

"Then he was suddenly transported off of the earth. What he could not tell was whether or not it was real or just images planted in his brain. They were not in any sort of craft. Rather, they were just racing through space, standing side by side. He was taken on a tour of the solar system, buzzing Jupiter, Saturn and Uranus. The high point of it was when they hovered close to the sun. He said that it was not hot nor overly-bright in the least, as if They could block it all out. And then just like that, they were back in the woods."

"What do you suppose the point of that was?" I asked, puzzled. They had taken this man on a cosmic joyride and I could not think of any reason for Them to have done so.

"I haven't a bloody clue. All one can do is speculate. It might have had something to do with what he said happened next. Spooner was really bothered by one *feeling* that They put into his skull: there was deep sorrow for him. It was as if, he said, They were humans looking at an earthworm and there was sadness coming from Them. It wasn't sadness about the fact that Spooner was the worm in the analogy. It was sorrow about the fact that the worm had no concept of what the worm really was, that it had no understanding of the world proper, the universe or his place in it. He was really certain on that point: They did not pity his ignorance per se, They were sad for him because his ignorance and lack of perspective was his own fault, like humans have squandered the opportunity to *be more,* choosing instead to be less.

"To Spooner, it came tied to a feeling that he said must be what it is like to be told that you have a malignant brain tumor that can't be removed. The trip through space only served to make the situation in his head all the worse. Think about it; he has just found out that neither he nor we are the kings of the earth that we have so arrogantly assumed ourselves to be for ages, then he was blasted in the face by the news that his own bloody backyard is replete with wonders that we have made almost no effort to understand."

"Christ on a cracker." I said. "To have that entire ice bath just dumped inside of a person's skull all at once, right after seeing our solar system up close... that poor boy must have been rocked something awful." I mused. Part of me was so jealous, so envious of Spooner. I have seen many planets through a telescope, but to be right up against them, to sit on the sun's corona... that had to be soul-shaking.

"Oh, he was shaken to his core, for certain. He said it was like waking up from his worst nightmare, but that the feelings didn't go away as soon as he realized that he was awake, as is the usual." Dad adjusted his back, trying to find a more comfortable posture.

"The burns to his body were supposed to be some kind of proof of the encounter." He continued.

"Was it from being close to the sun?" I asked.

"Not at all. Spooner said that it was Klaatu's response to his feeling that if he told anyone about the incident or that if he delivered the message as directed, nobody would ever swallow it, he would be ridiculed without mercy and he'd get a psych discharge for dessert. He said that his body slowly rotated to one side quite involuntarily, as if he was a marionette. Klaatu partially raised a hand just before a very short pulse of intense light hit him. It was completely superficial and didn't hurt him at all, but Klaatu assured him that it was a message.

I thought his burn looked queer. I'd seen enough people who had been burned by fires, and several who had caught a few too many rads at Los Alamos and Nagasaki. Spooner's face looked unusual somehow. It was like a mild sunburn, but subtly different... dichroic almost.

"Anyway, that's about the size of that. The only other thing he told us was that he got the impression that the Klaatu whom was there that night was..." He struggled for the right word. "Conflicted. About what, he couldn't really say. But the lad was dead sure of it. That's what set my teeth on edge. Was the Klaatu conflicted because he was ordered to lie to Spooner about coming in peace or about Their true mission or something else?" Dad let out a sigh and took another drink. "Shortly after the interview, I landed on this; if Klaatu controlled everything in that meeting, then Klaatu deliberately let those feelings through. He wanted Spooner to know that something was making him uneasy. That again raises the pressing question of, *why was that feeling there?*"

"Well did the Brits get their lie detector test?" I asked.

"Yes, for all the bloody good it did. Spooner flat-lined it like a corpse, as predicted. It was all as real as planet earth to him."

"Did you guys ever figure out what Klaatu was on edge about?" I had to ask.

"Yes, I believe that we did. But that's for another day." He looked straight into my eyes and I could see that whatever it was that he was *not* telling me in that moment was really twisting him up on the inside. I no longer felt that he was gauging my reactions though. To the contrary, he seemed to not care. "Later." He said with a heavy exhale. He slowly began to look as though the weight of the wold had been lifted from his chest.

"Will you promise me, right now, that you will tell me the rest soon?" I did not want to have to prise it out of him later, after he had time to change his mind about breaking his security oath.

Dad's voice became low and soft, like a classic Clint Eastwood gunslinger character. "If I were to tell you that if I were to tell you, you'll wish that I'd never told you, would you still want me to tell you?"

"In for a penny," I replied earnestly and instantly.

He regarded me carefully, waiting for some twitch betraying insincerity that never came. His look changed to one of pride and satisfaction.

"Okay. You've got my word on it."

4

Same Klaatu, Different Utensil

I had gone over to Dad's to move his refrigerator away from the wall one day so that he could vacuum behind it. Apparently that was a critical task that I was unaware of. Dust accumulations reduce the heat transfer efficiency and increase the energy required to keep one's French vanilla ice cream from going all milkshake. Afterwards, mission accomplished, we sat down in his living room to a lunch of grilled cheese sandwiches and Earl Grey tea. I had to razz him about the refrigerator.

"Not for nothing, Dad," I said, "but why is it that you are such a tree-hugging eco-warrior these days?" He took a bite of his sandwich and began speaking as he chewed.

"Yeah, right?" He said with a chuckle. "What's the bloody point in that?"

That was not at all what I expected.

"I'm not trying to give you a hard time, but I mean, I get that there is a reason to care about the environment. I just don't get why it is that you are such a holy roller about it."

He wiped his mouth with a paper towel. "Remind me to call that college you went to and demand a refund on Monday." He said dispassionately. "It's a non-linear SPDE (complicated math), you tit. Every little bit could be the little bit that makes the difference. If you knew that the light that you left on at home this morning was the wasted sixty watts that caused the entire global ecosystem to collapse and end the human race, wouldn't *you* be red faced!"

I had honestly never thought of it that way, and yes, I felt stupid for my lack of consciousness. "Yeah, I would." I said, turning my sandwich over on my plate. "What triggered this?" I asked as I stared at a dill pickle spear. "Not the refrigerator thing, but the elevated environmental consciousness? It kinda came out of nowhere."

"Yes, it did." Dad admitted. "It was Them. They flipped the switch."

I looked up from my plate to see a man I had never seen before; it was as if he was a Buddhist monk in a UConn sweatshirt, face as serene as a Himalayan glacial melt pond.

"What did they do?" I asked.

He grinned slyly and bit into his sandwich.

"They had been popping up here and there since the Spooner incident, just as Klaatu had said that They would. The brain trust that drives the bus completely disregarded Spooner's revelations. They committed themselves to trying to figure out Klaatu technology. They scrambled fighters and set up pointless radar monitoring programs, they coordinated intel with a number of foreign countries that were also pointlessly chasing any bogey that the radar painted. Right now there is a plan afoot to put up a gigantic shield over the U.S. that would work sort of like a metal detector so we can pick them up that way.[8] Our people were even infiltrating nutter groups to try to reap intel, as if those idiots had any clue."

"Which idiots? The government people or the UFO groups?" I interjected. That made him chuckle.

"The UFO twits. We already know that the government people are collective-moronic; I.Q. is the inverse-square of the population.[9] At first I had nothing but disdain and contempt for UFO people. But over time I became much more empathetic and understanding. Those UFO types would come up with SWAGs[10] for every aspect of aliens: how They managed to travel through space, where They had secret bases, why They are here. It's like a bunch of bacteria trying to figure out how computers work. I guess that fits the worm analogy. But they are actually pure of heart and motive, most of them. They're just frightened and confused and doing their best to make sense of things they have less than zero hope of ever comprehending,

---

8 The HAARP program was actually carried out, although it was sold to the public as a program to study the Northern Lights. But if you saw it, you'd know what a pant load that story was.

9 This just means that the more people involved, the more stupid the group becomes. Think of it as a fraction. If there were just two people in the government, the "collective I.Q. of the government would be 1/2 *squared,* or 1/2 of 1/2, so 1/4. If there were 100, it would be 1/100th of 1/100th, or 1/10,000. The U.S. government has roughly 2.9 million employees, so... yeah.

10 SWAG is an acronym for, "Simple/Stupid Wild Assed Guess."

turning every possibility into actuality in their heads. It's the same way that any religion begins, really.

"Every one of their 'ideas'," he rolled his eyes and swirled his index finger in the air, "was based on humanity's state of the art. A staple of the nutters is that every new, advanced human invention or discovery had to be a gift from the Klaatus and what They are using. None of those knobbers understands how idiotic they sound. 'OH! The government uses super secret encryption! They must have gotten it from the aliens and the aliens must be using it. *That* is why scientists aren't finding any alien shows on the telly!'

"At first, they guessed that the Klaatus used nuclear power, because that was state of the art. Then they started using Star Trek sci-fi ideas as explanations; warped space time engines, matter-antimatter fuel and the rot. LASER technology? Obviously free stuff from the space gods. They thought that Klaatus were here to save us from self-destruction in a nuclear holocaust because that was what was worrying the entire bloody planet in that moment. Why else would there be so many sightings near our missile bases, they 'reasoned'? It never occurred to those simpletons that there were a billion other reasons possible, most of them much more elegant and logical. There were and are a few men and women, real scientists wedded to objective examination of evidence, but they were getting very scant opportunity to flex their intellects because real Klaatus leave no evidence. But I digress." He shook his head, grinning, and took a deep breath before continuing.

"If the UFO researchers had known about Spooner, they would have ceased all operations and gone back to watching cartoons in their parents' basements. Anyway, the environment? That came from Malmstrom in 1980."

"So Malmstrom was real." I said flatly.

"Yes, very much so. Klaatus were there, a lot. They made themselves known to the base, quite deliberately, over a decade prior and made numerous additional visitations. But in December of '80, there was an airman there, we called him Fork, and I have no idea how that moniker came about, so don't ask. Probably just some agent being cute. Fork had the same kind of experience that Spooner had; the voice that told him to go meet Them, the encounter with Klaatu, the whole nine yards, including the sense that the Klaatu 'speaking' to him was nervous... uncomfortable. They even burned him the same way. That's one of the ways that we knew it was legitimately connected to the Spooner incident. The other was the reason that I got called in. Fork said that when They flash-burned him, he was told to tell people that the spoon man had received the same *warning*, from the same entity, and that he, meaning this particular Klaatu, was returning to where the spoon man received it. There were sightings back in England immediately. Everyone from the bottom to the top saw that as confirmation."

"Okay, hang on for a second." I said. "What warning? You never said that Spooner received a warning." Dad sat there, cheshire grin, twinkling eyes, allowing me to twist in the wind for an anxious moment.

"That's because we didn't know that Spooner had received a warning. Spooner said nothing of it because he was unaware of it. Apparently Klaatu overestimated our cleverness back then. Klaatu left a message and we bloody well missed it. But with Fork, we puzzled it out, which is to say that we serendipitously stumbled onto it." He adjusted his seat, leaned forward and became more animated than I had seen in many years.

"Just like in the Spooner incident, we collected samples of blood and hair, but this time we also collected fingernail clippings, because one of his nails was noticeably, obviously and deliberately augmented. It had a pattern that seemed to be designed to draw our attention to it. We must have missed it with Spooner, and of course, after a few months he'd have grown new nails and clipped away whatever might have been there.

"The analysts in the lab ran all of the usual tests, but one of the things that they wanted to see was whether or not the molecular structures in any of the samples had been damaged, and if so, how. We didn't know how he was burned, whether by radiation or heat or some other means. Science had come quite a long way since Spooner's event, so we were hoping to find something, anything useful in the samples. When they used a laser on the fingernail clippings to take a spectrograph, there was a pattern emitted. When they cut the sample in half, both samples gave off the exact same pattern. No matter how many times they cut them into smaller and smaller bits, each fragment emitted the exact same pattern."

"It was a freakin' hologram!" I blurted out, shocked and pleased with myself.

"Boy we could have used you back then!" Dad chuckled. "It took us quite a while to puzzle that one out. When it finally dawned on us what it was, everyone was buzzing about it being a star map or some sort of codex of knowledge. It turned out to be somewhat less romantic and potentially far more worth while." He sipped his tea before continuing.

"It was a note from Klaatu and an official report, all in binary that took almost no time to sort out. Actually, it wasn't the full report; it was like the executive summary of a much larger report, but it was still hundreds of pages. It referenced chapters of the full report along with exhibits and references and all sorts of things that humans might include in an official report. What was stunning to us was that the full official report must have been tens of *millions* of pages long, because there were references to chapter numbers and section numbers that were seven and eight digits. That makes perfect sense if you think about it. Klaatu's official report is shared with the hive as complete thoughts. Klaatu probably has centuries of visual images, experiences and such in his brain that served as exhibits. If I wrote out everything that I have seen and experienced in the last week, it would fill several books. So he must have converted the summary to a format that we could digest and then zapped it onto Fork's skin and nails.

"Anyway, it was all in English and formatted so that our simple chimp brains could clearly understand it. The note that prefaced it essentially said that this Klaatu was part of an expeditionary team, just as Spooner had reported. This Klaatu can communicate with us, but everything that he communicates to us by mind linking is also heard by all of the others. It is like he is using an open radio channel that anyone can and does listen in on when he mind-links with humans. It is like the entire hive-mind is there with him. More eyes on the target, so to speak. That's why I said that *They* plant thoughts in human heads, rather than that this one particular Klaatu did.

"Klaatu had to physically burn this information onto Spooner and Fork, as that was the safest way to get the message to us without the other Klaatus knowing that he'd done it. It would appear that each individual Klaatu have their own personal thoughts that They can keep to themselves. They seem to have some level of personal privacy in many regards, however when beaming thoughts and vacuuming up information from us, it's public data. The hologram was secret and secure, with little chance of it accidentally being found by other humans. This Klaatu was authorized to tell Spooner what he had told him, but it was not kosher for Klaatu to reveal the rest of what was in the burned-in message."

I was gobsmacked, bursting with anticipation of what was to come while simultaneously terrified because I knew it was some kind of a warning.

"Did you get to read it? The whole thing?" I asked hungrily.

"There were only three people on earth who actually read the entire thing, and I'm the only one who is still alive." He said. "Everyone else who knows about it, they only know it because we told them."

"What happened to the other two?" I asked before I realized that I probably didn't want to know the answer.

"They are no longer with us." He said solemnly.

I let it go at that because I didn't want him to get sidetracked from the contents of the report.

"The note said that there is a rule amongst the Klaatu about not interfering in any way with any entities that They encounter throughout the universe, much like the Prime Directive of Star Trek lore: superior races ought not screw with the lesser ones, nor give any material assistance to them. Were the other Klaatus to find out about him giving us the note and report, he would probably be viewed as having violated the rule. That implied, of course, that They travel the entire universe, not just the galaxy, which left us decidedly agog." My father took a long pause and had another sip of tea.

"Bugger me!" I said, breathlessly. "I don't know if you know this, but the universe is what scientists call, 'very, very big.' How can they ... What do they do, travel for millions of years?"

"Monty Python. Very good!" He said, smiling. "I'll get to that later. Klaatu's note said that he believed that he was not violating the rule, however. He was simply telling us, as a friend, things about ourselves that we *need* to know. He had been watching us for over ten thousand years and had developed an affinity for almost all life on earth. He was especially fond of domesticated dogs and the relationship that we have developed with them. Klaatu said that relationship bodes well for us.

"He said that he felt bad for us because we are still enslaved by time. Time really means nothing other than relationships between things that change, *if at all,* in only one direction, and that we are clever enough and knowledgable enough right now to figure that out. We had no idea what he meant by that. The galling part of that juicy tidbit is that nobody did a damned thing with it. We were given a gigantic hint about time and we just tossed it in the bin." He stood, stretched his legs and back, then returned to his seat.

"He also said that we need to broaden our minds, that we are limiting ourselves. He said that the report was written in English, and that will make many small minds suspicious. But the actual report is not written at all. As I said, it is all in his mind and will be transferred to the Klaatus that way, to all of Them at once. They have no languages per se. They have thoughts and ideas, much as Klaatu placed them in Spooner and Fork. He simply burned the report onto Fork in the manner most likely to be understood by his intended audience." He adjusted his aching back again.

"We shouldn't allow small minds to discourage our curiosity nor our understanding. People will question how They can move across vast distances, how They can maneuver and accelerate as They do, etcetera. Those small minds are bound by what they *think* they know. What we *actually* know is very close to nothing, and as I said, even when we are handed hints that might answer critical questions, we dispatch them like used tissues." He refilled his tea cup and reclined in his chair. "I'll tell you this much: They never use Einstein-Rosen bridges to travel through space."

"That's not terribly surprising, actually." I said with confidence. "Those things sound good on paper, but they strikes me as highly impractical as a means of travel... if you can even go through them at all."

"Klaatu intimated that the way that they travel so far so fast is based on something that requires far less energy and engineering than puckering the daylights out of spacetime. I just wish that the blasted spaceman had bothered to tell us what in the bloody hell it is that they actually do. But then, we know why he didn't tell us: that would clearly be giving aid and interfering."

"Yeah, that would definitely cross the *interference* line, especially if it gave some people an advantage over others, which it obviously would." I said, satisfied with the explanation.

"Yes, that is part of it." He said, chagrined.

I stood up and began to pace the room. That sometimes helped me to think. "Was that all of it, the note?" I inquired.

"The only other things that he said in his note were, '*You need to try harder to be better,*' and that he hopes to continue observing us for another thousand years." Dad let out a long sigh. "I felt really bad because I never got to meet him, to commune with him. I would have loved to have been able to ask whether or not the Klaatu ever contacted people like Socrates or Siddhartha, not that They have ever felt obliged to answer questions that humans have. But if he had, that would track. Lots of what Klaatu said mirrors several name-brand philosophers throughout history. It would be nice to know whether or not those people got any input from the Klaatus. That would certainly explain Their lack of interest in helping us, if we have been ignoring Them and their advice for thousands of years." He looked pensive for a moment and then chuckled. "I think I'd like that Klaatu. He almost seemed to have a bit of cheek about him."

"How so?" I asked with a quizzical look.

"He ended his note by signing it, 'Klaatu'." Dad said with a beaming grin.

5

The Report

At that moment I was so focused, so locked in and locked on, so curious, that I felt that I had to keep the conversation going.

"So, what about the report? What did the report say?" I asked. Dad's face and shoulders drooped, hard.

"Yeah, I was getting to that." He drew a deep breath and held it for a five count. "In for a penny, eh?" He asked sheepishly.

"Oh, absolutely!" I answered without so much as a thought.

"I'm afraid that it contained a lot of the answers that nobody really wants. The consequences of it were ... probably not what Klaatu intended, either." He contemplated his hands. "They *have* been coming here to scout out our planet. That is no lie. It is a one-hundred percent reconnaissance job."

"Then why in the hell have they been watching for thousands of years?" I shot back. "They ought to be able to learn everything important in a lot less time than that."

"Remember, a thousand years is time. Time doesn't matter to Them. For all we know They have been here ten minutes. We came to a consensus though. We think that

They can only *stop* time, or move and exist in such a way that what we think of it as time is standing still, or close enough to it that it doesn't make a difference. We are not thinking about it like in relativity theory. In relativity, time slows down for those things that are in higher energy states and speeds up for those in lower ones. Klaatus seem to be able to move without time changing very much for *anyone, anywhere*. Going backwards in time is probably off of the table though. It was the comments Klaatu made about time really just being a relationship between things, changing *if at all* in one direction, that lead us to that conclusion. If time is about changing relationships, going backwards in time, at least in the Orwellian sense of it, would not work. Maybe quantum mechanically you can do it to a few particles at a time in isolation, but for a person to go back in time to kill Hitler would require reversing all of the relationships of all of the particles in all of the universe. Besides, killing Hitler would not improve our lot one iota."

"I guess that makes sense." I said, thinking for a long moment. "That adds up, because if you merely wanted to go back in time one year, you would have to move the earth back to where it was in space, and where it is in both space and time is based on the relative positions of ... well, everything." I was more satisfied, although I didn't quite know why.

"That also means that all of the fanciful 'multiverse' codswallop doesn't exist." Dad said calmly. "There are no 'parallel universes' where there is a dumb Einstein or a genius Steven Hawking.[11] Our entire reality is trapped inside of these three physical dimensions and they are inextricably linked to time within those three physical dimensions."[12] Dad said with resignation.

"So, why are they scouting us?"

"This report was labeled, 'Phase Three,' so we surmised that there were previous phase one and phase two reports, probably tens of thousands or even millions of years ago. He referenced the dinosaurs as being the tail end of phase one, and the 'rise of intelligent life,' as the beginning of phase two."[13]

"Wowww!" I blurted out long and drawn, like the awestruck child I suddenly realized that I was. "I guess we really are way behind."

"That's the truth of it. They seem to have been able to cross the universe for at least one hundred million years. Either that or maybe a more local race visited here long ago

---

[11] Dad had a real problem with Hawking. He thought that Hawking was an overrated poster boy whom was being used by the physics intelligencia to sell books and elevate the profile of an astrophysics specialty that was based mostly on assumptions and guesswork.

[12] This was by far the most important thing that Dad hit upon, yet the gravity of it, no pun intended, only dawned upon me much later. Check out the Afterword for a brief discussion.

[13] We call this transition point, "The K-T Boundary." In our minds, it is the day that a giant meteor struck the earth and killed the dinosaurs along with *almost* everything else. K-T stands for the Cretaceous - Paleocene, because Cretaceous does not begin with a "K" and Paleocene does not begin with a "T". Go, team human!

and then merged with the Klaatu, adding their knowledge of us to the collective.

"But here's the sixpence in the Christmas pudding." He took a deep breath and held it for a five count. "*They think that we're done*, that intelligent life on earth is about to end. Their expeditions are becoming more frequent and overt because there is a land rush on. They have no reason to hide and no reason to help. Divvying up the corpse is what it's all about. We were so preoccupied with worrying about a never-existent alien invasion that we overlooked what was really going on. They are just waiting for us to kill ourselves, and now that we seem to be hell bent on doing it, They're making plans for earth, post-human life. Earth is most likely going to be a rest stop and vacation oasis on the interstellar highway, or some such rot."

"Is that why They spend so much time monitoring our nuclear facilities? Because They think we are going to blow ourselves up?" I asked.

"Not at all!" He said with almost pleasant surprise. "First of all, They lollygag around military bases with nuclear weapons because the bases are so bloody secure. It makes sense if you think about it. What better place to remain unbothered by snoops than a place where humans provide a barrier that prevents other humans from trundling about?" He said as he considered a biscuit. "Bases even have built-in techniques for cutting out passive snooping by other countries. Second, even if we nuked ourselves into ash, many mammals and birds would survive. Dolphins? They'd make it. Same with the primates and most of the wild animals in Africa, the Amazon... life would go on and new intelligent species would arise, according to Klaatu. In that case, they would leave the planet alone and just wait to see what happens next. They've seen that movie before on many other worlds. No, They actually have no concern about nuclear war. They also made reference to being able to fix things up after we are gone, even if there needs to be nuclear waste cleaned up. They said that all environmental imbalances can quickly be remediated with nearly one-hundred percent efficacy, in the event nature doesn't self-correct things in a timely manner."

"So what is it that makes them think that our collective goose is cooked?" I asked.

"That's complicated, so try not to get ahead of yourself with any one thing that I tell you. The gist of it is that humans are too arrogant and narrow minded for our own good. We fail to recognize our responsibilities to each other. We fail to recognize our obligation to the other intelligent species we cohabitate with. We fail to recognize our role as stewards of the planet. Every animal on this planet depends upon our *conscious benevolence*. Instead, we give them thoughtless selfishness. If humans weren't here, *all* of the other species would thrive. We are the disease that is going to kill earth."

"And when you learned this, that was when you became an environmentalist?" I asked.

"I'm not an environmentalist." He said bemusedly, as if he was an innocent child accused of nicking a cookie. "I just stopped being a gormless prat! I realized that every action I take has consequences. I've known Newton's Laws since I was a schoolboy. I just didn't interpret them as broadly, as philosophically as I should have. Every action has an *equal and opposite* reaction. Our satisfaction comes with a balance. Everything comes with a balancing force. The universe is just a big spreadsheet, and everything balances out to zero in the end."

"Well then, why aren't you a vegan?" I asked as politely as possible. I was trying to figure out where the jagged borders of all of this were located.

"I didn't become a vegan, but I did cut out eating cows and pigs for two grand reasons. Farming them is so damned awful for the planet. The report emphasized our total disregard for the cumulative and long term effects of *everything* that we do. It said that we are utilitarian, reactionary, short-sighted, that we subjugate our intellects to our emotions and that we do what we want, what feels good, rather than doing what we *should*, what we know to be right: things that best assure the long-term survival of the human species, our little ball of dirt and the other life on it. Maintaining the ecosystem that sustains us is imperative, yet the most intelligent beings *in this part of the galaxy* act like complete dolts. Besides, nobody *needs* to be a bloody vegan! We just need to be careful about how much damage we do farm-raising meat. Nobody needs to eat pork and beef every day, but we over-produce them and make our lot in life worse for it.

"On top of that, the report says that we are unenlightened because we kill our brethren." He took another sip of tea. "Initially we thought that he was talking about war and homicide, but as we read more we realized that he meant other mammals. That entire branch of our family tree is made up of *nothing but* highly intelligent creatures. In our arrogance, we choose to overlook this truth and to lie to ourselves, declaring ourselves to be their superiors and masters, entitled to kill them for our own selfish desires, simply because we use silverware and wear shoes.

"It doesn't help us that three-hundred thousand year old codswallop is stuck to the bottom of our intellectual shoes as '*holy rationalization*' for what Klaatu called 'the sociopathic genocide against our brothers and cousins.' The report points out that we do not have a single thought about how beneficial working *with* our brothers and cousins would be. Seemingly *every* Klaatu civilization has figured out this collaborative strategy and its benefits. They have developed strategies for integrating animals of common ancestry into Their culture. Monkey brains may be less capable than our own, but if we had ten million of them working in concert, all of them sharing their experiences with us, we'd gain some significant benefits. Giraffes and elephants can apparently tell us more about nature than we have figured out. Hell! He even said that we have no ability to, nor interest in, understanding plants. *PLANTS!* We don't realize that they can communicate! That is how and why *They* are visiting *us,* and not the other way around. It would seem that many other worlds have only been able to make it to *permanence* because of what the 'higher' beings learn from the 'lower.' At least the indigenous peoples of the world retain a modicum of respect for non-human life."

There was a long pause as those gems rattled around inside of my rock tumbler. Plants can communicate. What the hell? We can learn from monkeys, giraffes and Elephants! That is simultaneously nuts and sane. And then there was...

"Did Klaatu actually say that humans have had religion for three-hundred thousand years? Did I hear you correctly?" That sounded not right to me.

"Yes. The report said that there is evidence of it that we have not found yet but that we most likely will. They know of it because they could get into the heads of the creatures that pre-date us and those of the lineages that went extinct or that were subsumed by homo sapiens.[14] He says that they all developed notions of the soul, afterlife and powerful deities."

I was flabbergasted. I just could not wrap my head around this, so I scratched a quick note and then tried to get Dad back on track with what he had been saying previously. He obliged.

"The report draws extra-special attention to the fact that *humans can't even work peacefully and harmoniously with each other!* That seems to be one of the most damning assessments. Some people *know* and can *prove* how we are self-destructing. Unfortunately, too many other people believe that their selfish interests and baseless beliefs make the rational proof invalid and refuse to acknowledge it or take action. They don't want to give up their power or

---

[14] They may have found it. *"Ancient Human Relatives May Have Buried Their Dead"*
https://www.smithsonianmag.com/smart-news/ancient-human-relatives-may-have-buried-their-dead-180982308/

position. Klaatu never called us pathetic, but he might as well have."

"That's some pretty militant Marxist, eco-warrior, Kumbaya sounding rhetoric." I said jokingly. He half laughed with an almost dismayed resignation.

"It's no more 'rhetoric' than relativity, evolution, biology, maths or any other systems of knowledge that are based on observation, testing and falsifiability." He said. "The report said that one of the big reasons we are not worthy of an intervention is that most humans are so wedded to ignorance and superstition that collectively, we have but a minuscule hope of saving ourselves before the other shoe drops. Even if They were to intervene, the inertia of our stupidity would almost certainly not yield.

"It said that from a probabilistic standpoint, the 20th century should have been *the* period during which we realized the things that were most apt to destroy us and that we should have begun to address them then. Every intelligent world has their version of our 20th century. People start to become scientific, analytical. Then industrialization occurs. Next, the discovery of the nature of matter is made. But then the split occurs: some species recognize and deal with the harmful effects of progress and the consequences of their advancing mastery of nature, others do not. Humans did in-fact recognized almost all of the harms. Then we *deliberately and wantonly* ignored them. Sometimes we even doubled-down on stupidity."

"So, I'm guessing that Klaatus think that religion is the cancer that is killing us?" I asked half-heartedly.

"No and yes. It's more complex than that. They had a lot of very complementary things to say about religion. Religion, Klaatu said, is not inherently harmful. It has its place. It has purpose. It can provide moral lessons and reminders. But those are limited in both scope and duration. Humans take religion out of bounds." He adjusted his recliner to an upright position, twisting his back from side to side.

"Religion is something that is common to all species that evolve to create societies based on thinking. Smart, curious people want sure answers. When we aren't equipped to come up with actual answers, we fabricate them, creating religions, myths, legends, fables, what have you. It provides temporary comfort, an absolute set of answers, false though they may be. It can protect us from our ignorance. Ad hoc as it is, it is also perfectly utilitarian, in its place.

"Ants have societies that are based on biologically engrained traits, their actions are triggered by hormones and such. They are free of the burdens that hinder humans, but they have maxed out their potential for growth. Our potential is *boundless*. We just have to survive as a species. Religion is one of the main reasons that we made it out of the stone age. The report said that it was religion that largely allowed us to stop killing each other so much and to work together more. Our use of it was typical of that on most other worlds inhabited by intelligent species. A set of guiding moral principles uniformly applied across a society is likely a necessity, as he referred to it as a *highly* statistically significant factor in reaching permanence; not just to survive an age, but to reach *permanence*.

Unfortunately, when mishandled the way that we've done, something very good turns into something very harmful."

"What's permanence? You keep saying it like I'm supposed to know what that is. Oh, and don't ask why you paid for college." I quickly interjected. He rolled his eyes.

"It's like when you are starting a fire." Dad said, pretending to rub two sticks together. "You get a spark into some tinder material. That is what new life, life in the primordial ooze, is like. You blow into it to feed extra oxygen so that it gets sustainable, which is like crawling out of the ooze and being able to seek out food rather than having to wait for it to come to you as runoff draining into your pool. Even after the tinder catches, you still need to care for the fire, giving it kindling and oxygen until you have a fire that is sustainable for hours at a time and requires minimal maintenance."

"That's permanence?" I asked. "Because that seems to be where we are at right now."

"No it is not, and no, we are not. Humanity is still just a little campfire that is burning along, trying to survive whilst confined to our little fire pit, burning up our resources, competing to be the campfire that controls and burns the most fuel and oxygen." Dad chuckled. "Permanence is like when the fire in your camp site grows into a forrest fire. Embers fly off and start other fires. Fires merge together, split up, migrate and augment. On an extremely large planet, the fire would never go out, it would simply grow and change as a self-sustaining thing. As it spreads from place to place, the burned areas re-grow until the fires eventually circle back to the place of origin, starting the cycle over again. We are very far from getting out of our little fire pit.

"Where it all broke down for us was clear to Them. They have seen it so many times before that to Them, it is obvious. It's like when a person is addicted to drugs; if you leave them to their own devices, the scenario tends to play out according to statistical rules and most often it is not a happy ending; overdose, ruined lives, death. We are like that average outcome.

"Humans used religion for two main purposes: religious leaders used it to control others *for their own advantage* or to *maintain a status quo.* Religious leaders all became addicted to the power of controlling others almost from the word 'go'. This basic, natural and seemingly near-universal concept that allows intelligent species to survive beyond their primitive infancy was exploited by some people to advantage themselves and to enforce their naive, ignorant views of reality. The Qur'an, Bible, Gita, Torah, Guru Granth Sahib, Tripitaka and even the Book of Mormon... all great stuff according to Klaatu. Books Choc-full of great ideas, compendia of accumulated human wisdom they are. It is how these theologies were employed as a yoke rather than a teaching tool, how they were converted from aspirational and metaphorical principles into absolute, inviolable laws enforced by an elite class, that set us on the path to extinction.

"When evidence is developed that proves that the high priests are wrong comes about, what do they do? They deny it. They dig in their heels and stick to their false interpretations. They declare the scientist to be evil, heretical liars who must be silenced. Ask Giordano Bruno how that feels."[15]

"Rigidly clinging to traditions simply for the sake of saving face or maintaining control are the hallmarks of any institution, religious, scientific or otherwise, that is exceptionally harmful to the survival of a race. For example, religions that continue to enforce the belief that if you marry outside of your tribe or your 'race' you are going against some universal law? Ancient idiocy that once was marginally justifiable but is laughable in the face of what we know about the advantages of genetic diversity. Never eating swine? *Great rule* three thousand years ago when you could kill half of a tribe with undercooked pork stew! Today, that shite is just ignorant.

"Clinging to the idiotic isn't the heart of the problem though. It is the unwillingness of humans to *honestly* examine their beliefs, to question them, which is the unforgivable sin, pardon my humor. Klaatu said that it is a universal fact that if a people evolve and their thinking does not, they will extinguish themselves. Not may. *Will.* Don't miss the meta here, either. This clearly applies to political theory, social theory, theology, psychology... *EVERYTHING!"* Dad's passion was obvious, in a way I had rarely seen.

"As an aside, the report does says that the Mormons are actually the best of the bunch, small comfort that it is. Klaatu said that the Mormons evolve their thinking

---

[15] 16th century polymath Bruno thought that the stars were just suns with planets orbiting them and that our sun was not the center of creation. The Catholic church burned him alive.

relatively quickly. He actually called Brigham Young out by name as a glimmer of hope. Young, 'acknowledged the obvious structural flaws in their foundational concepts and effectively dealt with them in a manner that was less ad-hoc than any other human theology.' That's not saying much, but it's something. Klaatu was most hopeful about how Young's followers actually accepted the evolving theology. For our species, that was a one-off that should have set the standard." He poured more tea for the both of us.

"So religion is the problem when it comes right down to it?" I asked again.

"It isn't quite that straight forward. Religion was just the first domino to fall. It habituated us into becoming all too comfortable with what the report called, '*unearned authority*.' Any wanker who can quote words from a single human-fabricated document can become a social 'authority' who is beyond question on most of our planet. We 'learned' to relinquish our intellects to the unearned and unjustifiable authority of the priests and their made-up books. We then socially enforced the spread of that surrender. That ties back to our need for the comfort of thinking that we know things for certain, our need for light in the darkness, our fear of the unknown, our desire for stability. Anyway, those who exploit their positions diminish what Klaatu called the 'collective intellect' of the planet.

"Holding religious authorities on the same level as scientific authorities was another step toward our ultimate demise. Klaatus have seen it *millions* of times before. Using religion as a basis for moral value judgments is great. It's normative and is fairly easy for people to get behind, for the most part, so long as there is a *willingness to adapt to new knowledge*. Not ideas. Not new made up, ad hoc bullshit. *Knowledge*. But taking action or refraining from taking action based upon the words of men pretending to talk to gods... based upon edicts that clearly defy rationality, institutionalizing them and using social pressure to perpetuate them in the face of overwhelming, falsifiable evidence... that is tantamount to suicide for any intelligent species."

I was agog.

"The report talked about God?" I asked with appropriate reverence. I was hoping that there might be some hint as to the existence of deities. "Way to bury the lead if it did."

"Yes, it did. Essentially it said that we are nowhere near the point where we can even begin to grasp the real concept of god, well enough what 'god' actually is, how god works. God didn't create us in his own image. Humans created gods in *their* own image. It is our pretending to the ability, and the willingness of most people to blindly follow the untestable that are the problems. Blind faith is, universally, suicide.

"It described highly religious humans as, 'the most dangerous creatures, who promulgate ignorance, counterfactualism, hatred and the abandonment of all that makes humans special.' Look at the numb nuts who become radicalized Islamists. Their brilliant theology was completely perverted by a bunch of arsehole Imams with axes to grind. Suddenly you have armies of suicide bombers doing the dirty work of the cowards in charge. If we had just kept religion in its place, kept it in perspective, been honest about it, *evolved it,* that would have appreciably changed our trajectory.

"Races that reach permanence have a critical period where they realize that religion has its place, but that it is limited. They understand that the theory of evolution does not undermine god any more than maths do. If anything, maths and science are tools to help us *find* god. Humanity is very nearly at the end of that critical period. We are not the first race to fall into the trap, but statistically, we are very unlikely to survive the consequences if we don't take meaningful corrective action soon.

"The report also mentions that our theology is actually a powerfully positive thing for many *individuals,* and that it is this aspect of human religion that is unique to earth. The use of theology as a band aid for our perceived personal deficiencies is actually a favorable thing, and something rarely seen throughout the Klaatu's experiences."

"Would you clarify that, please." I needed something more concrete in order to understand his meaning. "You mentioned something like that before and I meant to ask."

"Alcoholics use religion as a tool to give them hope and strength, even though they have all of the strength that they need within themselves. Starving refugees in war zones do the same, as do political prisoners, crime victims, professional athletes and rice farmers. We use our concept of gods to access the inner strength that we only *think* that we lack. The irony, *expressly acknowledged* by Klaatu, is that humans largely believe that we lack strength because religions falsely made us believe so; to believe that we are impotent against the caprice of omnipotent deities who are benevolent parents and simultaneously malicious, vindictive arseholes. *That*, Klaatu says, is humanity's reflection of themselves: we want to be good but we default to douchebaggery. The report says that is part of the recurring theme of humanity's failures. We exploit each other by making each other feel small, deficient, bad, worthless... and then we try to sell each other a salve, be it holy salvation or mascara or weight loss drugs. In our hubris, we created religious lies that tell us that we are separate from and superior to the other residents of earth, even from our fellow humans. *We have dominion over the earth and the life upon it*, we lie to ourselves. Using human made religious lies past the point of their initial usefulness in order to justify harming other earth residents, waging holy wars, justify the killings of our brothers and cousins, to rationalize our misdeeds like slavery and subjugation... that put us on the path to perdition."

"Wow. Ain't you just a ray of sunshine." I said. "So, we are definitely fucked? Not *proper fucked*. Boned?" I asked.

That made Dad smirk again.

"We have a *non-zero* survival probability, for what that's worth. That was the point of Klaatu taking the risk of breaking the rules, methinks. Any chance is better than none. We have a tiny chance. Minuscule, actually. But compared to zero, it's infinite. That's why I'm not going full hedonist. That's why I'm doing what I can to help."

"By vacuuming behind your refrigerator and riding a recumbent bike?" I asked sarcastically.

It was like I had farted in church; he just stared at me in silence, not even appearing to breathe, waiting for me to say something smarter to keep him from blowing a gasket. I was getting very uncomfortable by the time he finally broke the silence.

"No, child," he said, quite calmly. "I am risking having my fucking brains splattered all over these walls in order to tell you the truth so that you can do something about it. Our current leaders, political and religious, seem to have either condemned humanity to its fate or are so deeply in denial that they refuse to act. Hell, they won't even to *talk* about it. Either way, this is our moment of reckoning. What do you reckon that you should do about it?"

6

Fitness Test

"And then there is money." Dad was back in the kitchen, putting on another kettle of water for even more tea, after a comfort break. "I have no damned clue as to how that one is going to get sorted."

"What about money?" I asked.

"It turns out that money really *is* the root of all evil, so score one for Paul the Apostle. We have fallen into a horrible trap with money, and once again, we are just one of millions of races throughout the universe who fell prey to it." He went about his tasks in the kitchen without elaborating upon a thought that clearly required fleshing out. I was more than a little annoyed.

"What is this trap of which you speak?" I prompted robotically.

"Our theory of earth-life evolution is, according to Klaatu, absolutely correct. Humans don't have all of the details and mechanisms of it down pat yet, but the report said that we have it correct enough, especially given our basic understanding of earth genetics, to be able to understand how idiotic we are being. We are simply choosing to turn a blind eye to the truth. Within the next four to five generations, it will be inexcusable."

"Please pardon me," I interrupted. "What does money have to do with evolution?" I was pretty sure that the connection was non-obvious. At least it was to me.

"Think about it this way. Humans were able to survive and rise to the top of the food chain with the sharks and polar bears because we had what it took to survive: smarts, cunning, strength, robustness, cleverness, will. It truly was the fittest who survived. We outlived ice ages and droughts, famines, floods, plagues and everything else that nature threw at us. We learned how to communicate both orally and in writing, through art and music. Our leaders were the best, strongest, and cleverest of the lot for thousands of years. That was because in order to be 'the leader' you had to prove yourself both in battle and through leadership. Leaders had to be able to protect not only their own sorry arses but also those of their family and clan. But even then, another strong person from the clan could challenge the leader and beat them in a fight. That only happened when the leader proved to be bad to his people or a toss pot who took actions that were deemed to be ludicrous. So whoever was in charge, they had earned it through strength and brains. Those sods procreated at ridiculously high rates. Think Genghis Kahn and his ten-thousand sprogs. The weak and the gormless... their gene pools dried up rapidly.

"But as we settled into communities and we became farmers, millers, cobblers, blacksmiths and what have you, money became a thing of *necessity*. It really allowed us to explode as a species. People could get highly skilled at one thing, like producing wheat or making swords, and then make enough money to survive without farming or hunting on the side. The ones who were really good and efficient could make extra money, survive in more comfort, have bigger dwellings, more food, more barges etcetera. Those people also made a lot of babies. Very quickly the people who were getting rich and doing a disproportionate amount of the breeding were no longer the strongest, best nor brightest. They were just highly adept at making swords etcetera and money.

"Rich people and their children are not necessarily either smart nor strong. In other words, they are not the *stuff* of survival. But they have money, so the vicious cycle propagates through the generations. If you just do the math it becomes clear that within a few generations, loads of people who should have died out because they are weak and moronic were spreading their genes, surviving longer and procreating more, simply because of the money that they had. Those dumb weaklings always had food and shelter. They could pay people to keep them alive by hiring guards and doctors. In a nutshell, money has thrown natural selection off of its rails by *making money a false proxy for evolutionary fitness*.

"It is easy to see today the results of that mistake. Look around at all of these scrawny, stupid one-trick rich people who breed like flies. Not a single one of them could survive on their own merits. Half of them can't even determine whether or not their yogurt is bad if it doesn't have an expiration date stamped on it. We have had presidents who were physically and mentally defective, billionaires who are lying, antisocial psychopaths, filling public offices with their hand picked sycophants. How did that happen? Money.

"Klaatu's report hit on this as another tragic blind spot that drastically diminishes the odds of our survival. We have a will to survive, that much has endured from the start. But now that money equals survival, the worst and the weakest survive far too often because they thoughtlessly feed the primordial survival instinct. They take over the leadership positions and have a disproportionate influence over the most important societal issues in ways that are advantageous to themselves and their kin, yet mostly detrimental to everyone else. Look at how long it took us *after* we figured out that smoking was deadly to do anything about it. That was money. Look at how long milk was pushed on us as a necessity for children. Again, money. Or how we make marijuana illegal because the alcohol lobby fears the competition. The liars and manipulators survive and spread their poisonous ways along with their genes.

"He didn't name names in his report. He was just very clear that we have been making awful leadership choices, all for the wrong reasons, and that we've been doing it for a very long time. Rich does not mean smart. Owning a large business doesn't mean that you make wise decisions or should be a senator. But way too many people all over the globe fail to follow that logic. They support and follow the rich because they assume that having more money must be based on intelligence and competence. That is why societal and environmental issues don't get adequately addressed. As Klaatu said, 'when money takes precedence over the survival of the species, the species does not survive."

"Well couldn't it be that natural selection is more about the survival of the *individual gene line*, each in their own way, and that nature will sort it out?" I asked. That made Dad smile.

"I'll bet Klaatu would love you. Even though They are probably at least one-hundred million years ahead of us and have studied millions upon millions of races, survivors and non, you question Their judgment." He looked sincere even though I felt like a chastised moron. "I mean it. He'd like it. It is *not* the questioning of Them that seems to perturb Them, it is not questioning Them.

"So YES, that is a way of looking at it, and a good way, but only when one is looking at early life and less advanced life forms. We are, according to Them, 'over that hump,' evolutionarily. We have survived, or at least we have made it past the *law of the jungle* phase, all credit to the K-T event. Klaatu referred to humanity as being 'post-*individual* survival,' like in the camp fire metaphor; we've made it past tinder and kindling and now we burn consistently as a fire in a pit.

"Klaatu made it explicitly clear that we are no longer individuals who need to kill or be killed in order to survive and propagate. We are in phase two of human evolution, where the survival of the entire species is now the priority over the survival of the individual gene line. For the vast majority of us, our genes are sufficiently well mixed and robust to keep this locomotive chugging along forever, provided we don't manage to derail ourselves. But swapping money for fitness has locked us into the animalistic practice of oppressing others for our own *individual* benefit in pursuit of this false proxy for evolutionary fitness. Sometimes it is overt, other times it is just systemic happenstance. Do you follow me?"

"Not really." I said with a confused look.

"Do you think that there is an evil cabal of old rich white men sitting in a room somewhere coming up with new and improved ways to keep people in ghettos?" He fired at me.

"Um, I sure hope not." Was the best I could come up with on the fly.

"No, there are not. There are rich people who want to become richer, planning ways to use society and its institutions to hold their money and power and to get more of it. Unfortunately, ghettos, super deficient schools, poor health care and other ills are an unintended consequence of their selfishness. Nobody set out to do that. But at the same time, not a bloody one of them set out to prevent it either, and that is another black mark on humanity's record. Any way you slice it, intentional or otherwise, it is counter to surviving to the next level of human evolution.

"In order to actually make that transition, our brains need to take charge and our base animalistic tendencies must be held in check by them. The vestigial cave-dweller mentality needs to come to heel. *The will of the intellect must prevail*. We exhibit little awareness of this life-or-death necessity. Money gets in the way. It makes people think that the pursuit of more money will make them more bulletproof against extinction. Once again, just like religion, we took something good and have abused it. We have employed a disadvantageous use of a good thing for far too long.

"This ties back to what They addressed about religions. We have the ability to think and coordinate and plan and collaborate. We should be able to collectively appreciate our special place on earth, make that adaptation and move beyond. That is precisely how these two factors, money and religion, conspire against us. Blind, unquestioning faith in witless pontification and self-serving rule making, turning off our brains in the face of obvious, objective evidence, the substitution of money for survival fitness, and then *giving* insanely huge sums of that money to the religious leaders... it's going to end up killing us all."

"And you say that Klattu mentioned that this was a common thing throughout the universe?" I asked, just to make sure I understood correctly.

"*Millions* of times. The report said that both the money and the religious phenomena have happened, together, millions of times. It seems that only the best species can work past it, and that is probably not us. Survival of the fittest is real. It is just that the meaning of 'fittest' has been improperly shifted mid-course by humans *to the wrong things*. The sods who use their wealth to employ violence in order to gain and maintain their control and survival... they truly are the lesser. They use their advantages over other members of their own kind, enslaving them and killing them, waging political, cultural and holy wars. I think Klaatu was disappointed and saddened by that. But not as much as They were by the fact that the wealthy, powerful and religious leaders all live like sultans while one in ten humans are malnourished to the point where even if we tried to educate them, they could nary develop to anywhere near what they are capable of achieving. We know this, yet the 'leaders' of nearly all human institutions do nothing to rectify the situation. They are too busy rolling around on the piles of money that we provide them with."

"But some non-human races have made it?" I asked hopefully.

"They have. However the statics aren't promising. The report said that amongst intelligent species who go through this progression, the odds of survival past phase two are less than one in five thousand. Of those that have made it past this hurdle, there is a seventy-five percent chance of making it to permanence."

"Only seventy-five percent?" I was surprised by the figure.

"Yes. Phase two of evolution is far from the end of things. Permanence is thought of as stage five. It makes sense. There are all sorts of natural disasters and seemingly random things that can snuff out a species or an entire planet. We need to work together, all of us, to guard against those potential harms." He picked up a biscuit, considered it, took a nibble and suddenly remembered something.

"What bodes well for us is that, of all of the survivors, over half of them are bipedal, engage in sexual reproduction, have domesticated pets and have some '*basic form of rudimentary communication*,' at stage two, meaning that they used printing and radio frequency. That part made me laugh, because so many of the nutters who 'research UFOs' think that Klaatus must be using radio waves to communicate. But like I said before, those types always think that whatever our state-of-the-art is, that must be what the aliens have. Those SETI people just don't get it, them and their quaint little radio dishes. They have pure hearts and empty heads, so I can't dislike them. We are a very long way from being able to eavesdrop on any of Their chatter. But you just wait until we figure out how to detect gravity waves. The 'UFO researchers' will suddenly become convinced that aliens communicate by gravity waves... but I digress."

My mind returned to something that Dad had said earlier, about not wanting to know.

"I'm glad that you are telling me about all of this, and I don't regret that you are. I'm not exactly sure what to do with it, but you're correct. Something needs to be done with it. People need to know. Obviously Klaatus are not going to land on the White House lawn or at Number 10 and drop off a manifesto, so someone needs to say something and do something. I'm really going to need to think on it."

Dad smiled.

"Well you're a pretty good thinker. You'll figure it out. You always do." He said kindly. He stood, stretched his aching back and did a little squat to loosen himself up.

"Just bear this in mind son: Nobody is going to throw you any ticker tape parade for relieving yourself on their picnic. Nobody wants to admit that they have been fooled, that they have been living a lie, even when it is almost everyone who has been duped for countless generations. The priests, professors and the politicians will *not* go quietly either. They will act rashly, violently, like cornered, rabid animals. This stuff is a threat to everything that they think they are.

If you try to take that away, or if you do anything that will undermine the system that got them to where they are, a system that keeps them in the comforts they are accustomed to, there will be harsh, hateful, vitriolic resistance. In the end, they are just sad, pathetic, delusional men and women who believe that they are something that they are not. There will be consequences. This is nuclear stuff, lad. Do not forget: *equal and opposite.*"

Dad walked over to the bay windows overlooking the wooded hills behind his home. "If you threaten the survival of the unfittest," he said with dramatic foreboding, "there *will* be hell to pay."

7

Why Him?

By December of 1998, I had a plan for dealing with what Dad had told me. I went to his house one morning to discuss it with him. One of the things that I needed, I thought, was solid evidence. I realized that nobody was going to believe a single word of his story unless there were some official reports or some physical evidence. I would prefer a bit of both.

I had poured over every UFO book that I could get my hands on. They mostly fell into two categories: anecdotes with no evidence (Betty and Barney Hill's story and Whitley Streiber's for example) and tales based upon allegedly official government documents. Anecdotal stories were useless because they lacked anything other than testimonial evidence, without question the absolutely worst evidence that there is. Attempts to manufacture proof by showing scars from alleged surgical procedures were convincing only to the uncritical. The document-based stories were always thrown into doubt because of some trivial detail that critics had with the format of the date on a report or the font used or the margin widths etc. That was actually for the better, because according to Dad, they were all, at best, delusions and fakes.

"There are no official documents." Dad said flatly, his face looking dejected. "We deliberately recorded nothing. Here was the 'thinking' that our government's finest employed, and I'm using 'thinking' in the broadest sense possible. This is *real.* We weren't trying to figure out whether or not it was. As soon as Fork's hologram was discovered, we all knew what a bloody global shit storm it would set off if the public ever found out. So the powers that be, in their collective wisdom, decided that the best course was to keep everybody calm until the end. Literally, the band is just going to keep on playing while the ship... goes... down. The alternative, anarchy, chaos and holy wars, was viewed to be the greater evil. It was cynical and shallow and illogical and an insult to the human spirit. It was also perfectly consistent with the reasons why the collective Klaatus will not aid us in any way."

"*Nobody* in either government thought that there was a glimmer of hope buried in there? Nobody thought that we ought to at least *try* to save our sorry asses?" I asked, incredulously.

"The three of us who originally read it thought that there was hope. We all thought that Klaatu thought so too, and that he was trying to give us clues to a fighting chance. The three of us determined that there was a need for immediate action, which scared the water right out of the upper echelons. But as I said, I'm the only one left alive, and nobody wanted nor was able to hear me. The panic that had set in within the halls of power was rapidly replaced by resignation, but in the immediate moments after word of what the report said made its way up the chain, the decision was made to bury it and to destroy all of the evidence. The Spooner and Fork tapes were torched along with the skin and finger nail samples, all of the reports... all of it. They even exhumed both Spooner and Fork and then cremated the lads, just to be safe. The sodding sons of bitches put both of them in the same goddamned oven along with four boxes of papers, tapes and film." Dad let out a big sigh and looked down at the floor pensively. "I actually cried as I watched it." There was a tear forming in one of his eyes.

I was shocked. Dad never cried. Not when Mom died, not when Grandma nor Grandpa died...never. I guess he and I both knew his threshold now.

"Fork had killed himself, or so officialdom has recorded. Bastards couldn't just make him dead, they had to say that he was heavily into drugs and died by autoerotic asphyxia. Cunts. Great way to cover a garrote job though. I think that the entire affair made the lad blow a gasket. He was going to leak his story eventually, so he had to go, or so said the king." He blew his nose, had a sip of water and composed himself before saying more.

"Reagan was the only one who was slightly moved by the idea of trying to survive, but he was surrounded by the most evil, rotten, selfish men America has ever produced, a bunch of antisocial ideologues hell bent on cold war stupidity. Credit to Ronnie, though. He eventually tried to plant the idea in the public mind that if there were a threat to humanity from aliens, we'd all work together to survive.

He just went about it in the most ham-fisted way imaginable."

I thought about that. I remembered Reagan's famous alien invasion speech at the U.N. in 1987. It made him seem like the senile nutter that he was actually becoming. I also remember how quickly the point he was trying to make got washed away, subsumed by the tsunami of illegal activities his clown car of rottenness was up to.

"How is it that you survived the purge?" I asked. "The other two who read the report died very shortly after it was discovered. You didn't. Is there a story there?"

Dad grinned. "We were *the* potentially leaky arteries that needed to be cauterized, and with all deliberate speed. That we three thought humanity ought to do something other than sit around with our thumbs up our bums made the twats upstairs twitchy as a meth head. That much was clear to me when I looked into the faces of the men who were there blatantly observing us as we watched the funeral pyre. The other two... they were desk jockeys. They had fuck all ability to hide their thoughts from their faces. To me, they were potential sieves. I played my tears off as sorrow for Fork, whom I had gotten to know rather well, then put on my best company-man face and said aloud that what was done was necessary for the good of the country. I guess that was why they tried to bag me last; I made them stew on whether or not I was a risk, at least for a tick.

"That's when I told the rat bastards that I had an insurance policy." He said slyly. "I told them that I had transcribed the entire report summary and had it tucked away somewhere safe."

"I'm not sure how that would have actually saved you. If anyone were to stumble upon it, they'd just think that it was the lunatic ramblings of someone who was off of their meds." I said.

Dad focused his death glare at my eyes, silently lasering my brain. "And you think that your old man was so dim as to have *not* realized that? I'm hurt, son."

"So what was your ace in the hole, DaVinci?"

"What do you think?" He said, straightening his posture to attention. "I told them that I'd nicked a piece of Fork's fingernail before they burned the rest!" His face was abeam. "I said that I had cached my transcription and the nail in a secure, remote location, just in case catastrophe struck. It was all very non-threatening, in the most subtly threatening sort of way possible. I phrased everything in the hypothetical. '*If* I had a hologram... *If* I had a transcript...' '*If something were to happen to me...'* Uncle Sam understood the risk of harming me; all of it would be sent to the New York Times and the Times of London."

"Holy crap!" I blurted out. "You intimated that you had committed a federal crime? I guess your bullocks are bigger than I ever realized!" It only took me a second to take the next step. "You had to be bluffing though, right?"

Dad just smiled knowingly, silently sliding into a memory he would rather forget.

"I had to do *something*. By that point the other two were MIA and presumed by me to be dead. I sussed out that I had to be next on the hit parade. Sadly for the company, they only sent one garden variety troll to neutralize me. Poor decision making is the hallmark of those wankers. I guess that they figured that with my bodged-up spine, I'd be an easy take down."

"THOSE MOTHERFU...!" I said angrily, enraged that they would try to kill my dad. "They actually had the temerity to try to take you out?"

"I assumed so. Like I said, the others had been *persona non grata* for several days. I was told that they had been transferred to other projects, but I didn't swallow that rubbish. I was paranoid for several sleepless days. But when the gormless tit showed up on my doorstep, quite literally, I just instinctively knew it was game-on, and I was well prepared. Ventilated the poor sod right there on my own front porch. Three in the 10X, double-tap center of mass and one insurance policy."[16]

"What the hell!?! You iced a dude? At home? With mother in the house?" This I had never in my wildest dreams anticipated. Dad was demure and came off as nearly nebbish. Nobody would ever suspect that he had it in him.

"Yes, I did. I had a suppressor. Your mother was asleep in the upstairs bedroom and was none the wiser. But the asset showed up dressed as a parcel deliveryman. Never even got a bloody word out to me." He said wistfully.

---

16 Practice targets that look like human silhouettes have rings on them indicating the number of points one receives for a hit. The 10-X rings are located just below the base of the breastbone and right between the eyes. The two shots to the chest are sufficient to end a person's life, but unlike in the movies, they usually don't just drop dead and can still get a shot off. That's why the third shot between the eyes was needed, to actually stop the assassin from killing Dad by shutting off the brain. That's an *insurance policy*.

"Weren't you worried that you'd just smoked the DHL dude?" I asked, hungry for details and insensitive to what was probably a nasty PTSD moment.

"Yes, actually I was. And she was a woman just before she became an ex-woman. They like to send women when they can. Very disarming." He sighed. "I pulled her inside before her knees even buckled, rifled through her belongings, verified that she was delivering tickets to the afterlife and then cleaned up. Tweaked my back something fierce, but adrenaline is nature's magic elixir.

"I went to work the next day, same as always, acting none the wiser. *That* was when I told them about the transcription and clippings I'd stashed. All very unspoken waving of the twig and snozberries.[17] They got the message and everyone played nice after that."

I stared at him in stunned silence, slack-jawed, head throbbing. First tears, then homicide. My reality was cracking ten ways from Sunday.

"Didn't think I had it in me?" He asked. "I was in the bloody war. I spent over a year in Europe slogging love notes and dealing with jilted lovers. The UK, Scandinavia and France are dotted with my PPK's handiwork." He said it the same way that one might list the trails that they have hiked.

---

[17] If you saw the original "Willie Wonka and the Chocolate Factory" movie, you may recall Wonka saying, "The snozzberries taste like snozzberries!" The author of the story, Roald Dahl, wrote another story, "My Uncle Oswald," in which snozzberries were revealed to be testicles. This is widely regarded as the sickest adult joke ever slipped into a kid's movie.

"What in the hell did you do with her body, the DHL lady's?" I was staring at his feet, numb, and can't even recall the look on Dad's face in the moment.

"With proper training and a bit of practice, one can become quite efficient at sanitation. Although the situation with my vertebrae forced me to employ some less than savory, slightly inelegant methodologies. Suffice it to say, I am ever grateful for Glad kitchen trash bags and Buck saws."

I was shocked and embarrassed. I never knew that he even owned a gun. I certainly never thought that he would use one. He was a glorified courier in my mind; a memo delivery boy. But I suppose that the things he was transporting during the war were valuable enough to create a sack-full of kill or be killed scenarios, especially in the midst of a hot war. But... I was ninety-nine percent sure that he was saying that he had to cut the body into pieces to transport it. I was *not* going to ask for confirmation nor details.

That was when I told him of my plan to release his story after he passed away. I would do it in book form and simultaneously sell the movie rights. If he had a chunk of the hologram, that would be *the* evidence that I needed for verification. I wanted to ask him whether or not he still had it, but decided against it for two reasons. First, I wasn't even sure that his claim of having it wasn't a bluff. Second, he was committed to the story being told to and believed by the public. If he had anything, he would eventually turn it over to me. I had to hope that he did not die without sharing it somehow.

"That sounds like a good plan." Dad said.

"I'll leave out the part about you topping the parcel lass." I said, almost apologetically.

"No, you most certainly will not!" He snapped. "People need to know the entire truth. These are some depraved, rotten hemorrhoids that we are dealing with. You cannot deny the public that knowledge."

8

Waste Not

"Do you know what the most valuable commodity on earth is?" Dad asked.

I felt like a school boy being asked a question by his professor, the professor having an answer in his brain that he wanted to hear, even though there were any number of possible answers that were arguably correct. In other words, it was a *Kobayashi Maru* scenario.[18]

"Did Klattu's report have the answer?" I finally asked. Of all of the wrong things to say, that was probably the wrongest, and I knew it as soon as it left my lips.

"Since when is answering a question with a question appropriate?" He queried over the top of his readers.

"That's facile. You asked a vague question that requires clarification." I tried to sound non-confrontational. I failed. He pursed his lips and dodged the barb. Very Jackie Chan.

"The human mind. There isn't a human brain on this planet that is worth less than all of the precious metals and gems buried on earth, and that includes people who we deem to be intellectually disabled. Each and every human mind is imbued with its own form of genius. Tapping into that genius... optimizing and maximizing it...that is the

---

[18] A no-win situation.

challenge." He said. "That was yet another part of Klaatu's report that really stung. It was a brutal, acidic indictment of humanity. Given that I'm certain that Klaatu was trying to aid us by leaking it, I took it as both rebuke and guide star.

"Critical thinking is the key to reaching permanence. They have determined that in order for an intelligent race to dodge evolution's many poisoned arrows, a *minimum* of 17.5% or about one billion, whichever is less, of that species has to have highly developed critical thinking skills. Humanity is pathetically below one percent."

"Wait wait wait!" I interrupted. "Five and three quarters billion people is the cut-off point at which one billion smart people will sustain any number of idiots to permanence?" I got a chill from head to toe.

"Think boy!" He barked at me. "First, it is not that it *will*, only that it can; it's necessary, not sufficient. Second, if you have the minimum number or percentage, that will actually grow larger, because smart begets smart. Third, *we* are on the cusp of six billion people on earth, and seven, eight and nine are coming fast. Klaatu presumably warned us of this the first time with Spooner, back when we were at two and a half billion people, which is yet another reason I think that he's trying to help us. We were coming up on the half-way point back then, and making negative progress. Klaatu must have panicked when he realized that we had hit four and a half billion but had done nothing to work on the problem other than to exacerbate it. He must have surmised that we missed the message the first time and so he hit Fork on American soil. Perhaps Klaatu was hoping that the U.S. government would, if independently contacted, make a wiser choice about disclosure or at least which course of action to take.

"We need to dramatically up our percentage of solid critical thinkers. I was certain that the American government would do the math and take action long before now. Why in the hell wouldn't they?" He yelled, anger ablaze in his eyes. "It is such an easy thing to fix and would give the United States a huge advantage in the survival race, not to mention geopolitically and economically. However, I suppose that's the larger point.

"According to the report, we squander human intellectual potential on a scale rarely seen throughout all of the universe. Our *biological brains* are some of the most capable that They have ever seen and by far the best in our galaxy. But we warehouse kids in bad schools, we poorly and generically educate them. We label them as *inferior* or *normal* or *gifted* or *superior*... we completely waste almost all of every person's intellectual potential. We deny access to education to most of our species, burning intellectual potential like so much coal by not even *feeding* vast populations of children, forcing them to work in factories or to pick through the leavings of the bins of others. It's humiliating. Just feed them and keep them healthy. That would get the ball rolling. Then educate them. Nothing radical, just the basics of self-learning and logic. Then give them access to as much as possible so that they can follow their curiosity. It is tragic that we don't."

"Hold on just a gall-dang minute!" I interjected. "In order for Them to be able to say any of that, They would have to have a pretty solid idea of what our maximum capabilities are."

"All too correct." Dad said with a hint of surprise in his voice. "They said that of all of the *biological* entities known to Them, we have the greatest intellectual capacity by a significant margin. But we are akin to a caveman who finds a computer and fancies it a great tool for crushing skulls, oblivious to a stupefying degree as to what we actually have. Worst of all, we think that we are *competent* to make judgments about who has potential, what that potential is and how to *best develop it*. We are decidedly not.

"The people doing the judging are holding others up to their own ego-driven self images and pathetically archaic notions. Doctoral programs have almost nothing to do with developing brilliance; they have been reduced to conformity factories. Arrogant prats tell young scientists that they are not worthy of academic recognition if they disagree with or dare to question their advisors' patently absurd views, ruining their careers and lives.

"The cultural and experiential biases built into nearly every education system on earth adds to the problem. Knowledge and logic are universal, yet we limit access to knowledge, we misrepresent supposition as fact, and we reward specious conclusions. The *academics* who create education systems actually undermine them with their mostly unscientific ideas. However, I suppose it's the same reason many societies still foolishly cling to class systems. They try to make themselves *feel* superior when in fact, *they are the problem*.

"The report said that our greatest minds, the ones we hold out as the pinnacle of genius; none of them are all that special. The Einsteins and Tchaikovskys of the world basically had environmental factors that triggered their growth and allowed them to excel, relative to other humans, anyway. Those boys would be considered garden variety under-achievers within all of the species who have made it to permanence. Everyone is different of course, in what catalyzes their genius, and how that mind-optimization manifests itself is wildly varied and most often unrecognized. But in the end, anyone can be a genius by our apparently laughably low standards. We have the ability to radically expand the quantity of true genius thinkers and to accelerate that process. We just squander the opportunities." He sat back down, kicked his slippers off of his feet and reclined in his chair.

"Klattu's estimation was that over ninety-nine percent of human intellectual capacity is either wasted or untapped. That has nothing at all to do with the old lie that people only use three percent of their brains or what have you. We use all of it. But it is like having a two-hundred watt light bulb and feeding it milliwatts of power. That we are blithely unaware of this is a tragedy that is directly linked back to money.

"We allocate a pittance of our collective wealth toward researching how to better educate our offspring, to developing methods to better draw out the potential of our people, to even educate them in ways that raise our overall intelligence. *Why?!?* Because the bloody sods with the money, including governments, believe that there is no profit in doing it, or at least not enough for them in the short term. Over the long term it is highly economically advantageous. But these greedy buggers would rather exploit the few people who become above-average on their own than intentionally create legions of creative geniuses who can literally wipe out hunger, cure diseases, and move us past the roadblocks that have held us back. Our desire to create nominally literate workers at the lowest possible price-point so that we can exploit them for maximum profit is the one thing that I thought really made Klaatu sad... or hacked off. I actually couldn't be certain." He lit up a cigar and took a puff.

"And then there is the fact that the average human has little to no time to assist in educating their offspring... we did that to ourselves. It is that global money trap again. We have embedded ourselves in an unsustainable paradigm where feeding our families is actually *harder* than it would be if we just hunted and gathered in a pre-industrial way. We could all home school our kids if we all worked together. It happens on almost all of the worlds that reach permanence. By the time Their children reach maturity They are ready for academies and colleges, fully prepared for educations that make our PhD programs look like an episode of Sesame Street." He sat in silence for a moment, transfixed by the patterns of smoke rising from his stogy.

"Here's an interesting aside. I read the report with two other people and each of us got something different from it, at least as far as how it made us feel. I thought Klaatu was angry with us for failing to educate each other. The other gent sensed sadness coming through. The lady thought it was melancholy. I almost think that the clever bastard embedded all of that in there somehow, and that it took a collective reading to most accurately interpret it. More eyes on the target, so to speak. That was my take on it, not that anyone gave a shite. In fact, I was actually *derided* for the suggestion. 'Do you think we should put this thing on the reading list of a goddamned book club?' My director had the bullocks to snap at me." He laid his head back against the headrest of his recliner and blew a series of smoke rings above his face. He appeared to me to be centering himself.

"I've come to believe that this report was really Klaatu trying to tell us what to do in order to dodge our demise. Do you follow me? He likes us. He showed us what our biggest problems are. He risked," Dad paused for a long moment, puzzlement upon his brow. "I suppose that I have no idea as to whether or not he risked anything!" He looked surprised at his realization. "Perhaps there's no consequence for breaking their rules, other than a loss of face, so to speak. Perhaps guilt. Probably not...

"That aside, you can see the problem here. Proper education is the enemy of those who exploit by fear, manipulation, disinformation and lies. Why do you think the Russians and Chinese suppress the free exchange of information and imprison academics? Why they live by disinformation and outright lies? Why their idea of education more like indoctrination reserved for the children of the party bootlicks? The commies are deemed to be inferior for those reasons amongst many others. Klaatu said that of all of the people on Earth, the Scandinavians and the Indians, both feather and dot, are the only ones who have a whiff of what needs to be done, yet even they are woefully deficient.

"But there was a reference he made to the races on other worlds who made it to permanence. They mostly do not have societal education for children, no public schools. They have institutions that teach their people two things only: critical thinking skills and *how to learn*. Once that's achieved, they provide limitless access to information so that everyone can soak in as much as they want from each other and on their own. It probably would help a lot if they could already do that mind trick they laid on Fork and Spooner. Those who so desire can attend those advanced academies I mentioned before in order to gain focused curriculums. Can you imagine what would happen if we did that here? Not the Vulcan mind meld thing; we have that capacity, but we aren't ready for it."

I made a mental note to follow up on that.

"The entire power structure of most of human society's institutions would dissolve like a sugar cube in a cuppa. All of the lies would become laughable, all of the truths would emerge. Priests, politicians, professors, parents... all of their codswallop would be laid bare, all of their fabricated authority revealed to be the Wizard of Oz... we would ask a lot more questions, because *nothing is beyond question*. This is a direct quote from Them: 'Survival to permanence requires that the notion of *taboo* be banished.' Klaatu phrased it as *'bad data in our calculus,'* the reliance upon unverified, or worse, unfalsifiable information in our thought processes and decision making. *Unverified* sometimes happens, especially when scientists are in their process, forming hypotheses and then testing them. But allowing the *unfalsifiable* [19] into our processes, that is a cardinal sin. People who do it are not even willing to raise the question of whether or not whatever it is they rely on could possibly be tested for accuracy. They just take asinine thoughts as given facts based upon faith. Until we stop basing our thinking on bad data, we will be headed in the wrong direction. Unless we *want* humanity to vanish, that is." He tamped the stub of his cigar out in the pedestal ashtray next to his chair and began to stand.

"Klaatus appear to *revere* intelligence, elevating the best, most capable, cleverest, curious and creative beings to the highest social status. It's pretty much the opposite of us, and something that we need to get right with. Our minds are our one and only true advantage and yet we have this infantile and animalistic approach to using and developing them." He grabbed his jacket and headed toward the door to go to a movie with me. "I can tell you this much." He said as he slipped on his leather loafers. "Throughout the universe, those who use their brains and who stop relying on bad data, they are mega-parsecs closer to understanding the divine than any earth-bound wanker pretending to talk to the gods has ever been."

"You said that we have the capacity to do the mind-locking thing. What can you tell me about that?" I asked

---

[19] "Falsifiable" doesn't mean what most people think that it does. It means that we *have the ability* to test whether or not something is true or false. There are no tests for some things (gods, magic), hence we can only accept them on faith. No amount of B.S. can change that.

him. "It almost seemed like you were trying to slip that past the keeper."

"We apparently are pretty close to realizing it." He said casually. "There was a reference to how our understanding of quantum mechanics and electromagnetism puts us very close to making that leap. But if we were to figure it out, it would be devastating, because we are emotionally incapable of handling the truth. Just imagine knowing what your wife *really* thinks. Now throw that into a bar full of pissed knuckleheads or a pitch full of football hooligans."

"No joke?" I was shocked that Klaatu would have tipped us to that. "Doesn't that seem to border on interference?"

"You are not wrong, in my estimation." He said with yet another sigh. "That little gem was reported in the context of how we limit ourselves through our assumptions, how scientists, the best ones we have, put on blinders to the possibilities. 'ESP cannot be real,' is dogma to them.

"But even Einstein fell into that kind of a trap, and more than once. The man was totally lucid with relativity, but then he started to question the logic and stumbled when he saw things in the math that his monkey brain could not grasp as possibly being real. He had to learn that the logic is woven into the universe and it is never wrong. Once we have good data, logic is incapable of telling a lie. When we see things that intuitively shock or confuse us, we need to reevaluate our assumptions, not simply disregard the logic because it conflicts with our beliefs.[20] That is what we usually do. In the end, Einstein got *mostly* right with it, but it took him time to rationally bury his emotional misgivings.

"He accepted his 'greatest blunder' and fell on his sword, even though he had not blundered at all, other than doubting the logic. He also fell into line on quantum mechanics, which he essentially discovered, even though he famously said that, 'God does not play dice,' meaning that our universe cannot be governed by statistical laws. It took him a while to get right on quantum non-locality[21] too, which he initially loathed simply upon principle, not based on the logic, which said that it is very much real. But that's what makes him great to us. He was able to mostly remain rational for the majority of his life."

"You used 'mostly' quite a bit. Anything to it?" I asked, certain that there *was* something to it.

"Very little in our universe appears to be absolute." He picked up the remote for his television, thinking that there might be a Manchester United football match on the satellite; he liked to leave football on for the cat when he went out. "There are probably some physical laws that are

---

[20] Paul Dirac and J. Robert Oppenheimer of A-bomb fame "discovered" antimatter in just this way: the math said that there are particles like electrons that have all of the same quantum values as electrons, just exactly the opposite. The logic did not lie. A couple of years later, Carl D. Anderson whipped some up.

[21] Put simply, quantum non-locality is a cause and effect relationship that happens not just faster than light, but *instantaneously*, regardless of how far apart two particles are. The math says that it is real but Einstein could not accept it... until he did, because it is real.

always true for us, but little else is universally absolute. You may have noticed that Klaatu's report speaks in terms of odds and probabilities. That's why. Einstein was *mostly* correct about relativity, both Special and General. He was mostly correct most of the time. However, I got the distinct impression that Klaatu hoped to impress upon us that if we discovered the blind spots in those theories, the false assumptions, we would benefit quite a bit."

9

Come On, People Now...

When Russia invaded and annexed part of Crimea in 2014, the world was on edge. Russia's Tsar[22], Vladimir Putin, whom Dad called "Vlad the Impotent," (something that I assumed was based on intel he was privy to) was playing with fire. Putin knew that if he moved quickly and broadly, there would be a huge backlash. So he played the long game and moved slowly, taking *kroshechnyye kusochki,* (small bites), believing that the world would do nothing to oppose him. Eventually, Putin believed, he could etch his name in the history books as the great man who restored past Russian Stalinist power and glory.

What his point of view overlooked and disrespected was the collective soul of the Russian people. The Russian people beat the Nazis on 'the Eastern front,' not Stalin. The Russian people kept themselves fed and safe, not Stalin. The Russian people endured the decades of failed communist/socialist economic policies and international

---

[22] Dad called him Tsar, so I used it to keep as much of his voice in the story as possible. His rationale was that Putin wanted to be a Tsar. He acted like one, grossly and obscenely enriched himself while his people struggled, never faced a fair fight in his life, imprisoned, killed and crushed any and all dissent, put in the fix for every election... If it walks like a duck.

isolation, not Stalin. Stalin was Russia's only real problem. Putin cynically and selfishly exploited the Stalinist myth to aggrandize himself, but at the expense of further divorcing the greatness of his people from the truth of history. That unvarnished truth says that the only power and glory Russia ever had was within the heart and mind and will of her people.

I went to Dad's to get his take on the situation and to help him paint his den. I knew that he had been in a bunch of high level briefings of late via some secure bunker's more secure video conferencing system. He was very old but still quite mobile at that point, although his back hurt him fiercely: he refused to travel farther than the military bases nearest him. I figured he had the skinny on, or at least the gist of, what the brass was thinking.

"He's going to try to take the whole damned country (Ukraine) eventually. He hates the idea of having anything approximating freedom on his doorstep. It's too damned easy for truthful information to bleed over the border and threaten his power. It's even easier for Russian citizens, toiling in a system that never did work for the people, to see a Ukrainian with a nice car and an iPad. 'How ya gonna keep 'em down on the farm after they've seen Paree?' "

"Do you think he's willing to risk the blowback from the international community?" I asked naively.

"My boy," he said, shaking his head, "there is no *international community."* His voice was thick with derision, hands flashing air quotes. "The United Nations is a swanny (toilet) of disassociated entities that pretend to get along whenever it suits the needs of some of them. It's a bloody laugh. The members can't get their heads out of their selfish arses long enough to do anything meaningful unless one of the power players stands to gain from it, like in Iraq. The Russians, Chinese, Indians, Brits, French and Americans all have diametrically opposed objectives, so good luck getting blood from that turnip."

"Well then, what is going to happen in Crimea?" I asked.

"Not a bloody thing! The West will grumble, but nothing will happen. When Vlad finally reveals his designs on all of Ukraine, we will cobble together another *coalition of the willing*, but that will all be for show. 'Ukraine has no oil,' as they say in the halls of power. And mark my words, the same thing will happen when the bloody Chinese run an anaconda scenario on Taiwan. The West's attitude is that if they want freedom, they can earn it on their own, with our weapons, of course. You don't want to deny the reelection-money deities at Lockheed their tithing. Those sods would go belly up without the government teat."

We shuffled out to the garage to escape the paint fumes for a few minutes and to retrieve another gallon of eggshell white paint, a staple of his generation. Heaven forbid they should have a little color into their homes.

"Do you know how many different races of humans there are on earth?" Dad was ever so fond of beginning conversations with questions. Many people found it to be off-putting, but having grown up with it, I knew that it was just his way. It made him feel quasi-Socratic.

"I have no idea." I replied. "My suspicion is that the answer depends upon who you ask. When it boils right down to it though, there's probably only one." That made my father smile with surprise and pride.

"Your instincts serve you well!" He said, channeling his inner ObiWan Kenobi. "We have a hardwired survival mechanism that is pretty universal: the ability to distinguish fine differences between things. It's actually a characteristic that distinguishes life forms. Most of them can tell a flower from a flame because if they can't, they go extinct. But humans have elevated it to a fine art. Our minds consciously and subconsciously catalogue the minutia of other people, parsing them into finer and more nuanced subcategories.

"Once we managed to extract ourselves from the wild, the primary threat to each person's life came from other humans. Think about it this way. One hundred-thousand years ago, if some other human approached you from out of the wilderness, there was no real way to tell whether or not they were friend or foe or traveler. Twitchy as we were, we became fearful of others, and rightly so, murder being what it is. As we moved into clans and then towns, we got used to being surround by scads of other individual humans, but we still innately feared the different people of the different tribes as well as the different amongst us. Race is an easy way to imagine that the human in front of you is different, dangerous, bad. We developed terrible ideas about each other, each group pretending to superiority, invoking superstition and religion to justify persecution, slavery, isolation, insularity and war." He opened the garage refrigerator and removed two bottles of San Pellegrino.

"The point of my little TED talk is that we created this ruddy *Song of Ice and Fire* without recognizing the underlying motivations; our primeval fear of the different metastasized. We took our skillset for distinguishing minute differences too far, and now we cannot bring ourselves to admit that we need to rein it in. We became fearful, suspicious, *paranoid* about everything different. We formed nations because we parsed people for all of the wrong reasons, and to this day we fail to make even nominal efforts to rectify the situation."

"Are there any non-wrong reasons for parsing people?" I asked him.

"Actually, there is one, or at least They seem to think so. It appears that They draw a line between Themselves and those who undermine the survival of intelligent races. That's it. Capitalism is fine, you just have to contribute back to the various species that afforded you the opportunity to exploit them, which is really all of them, hence the need for *conscious benevolence*. At least that is how I read it, and I have read it cover to cover, nearly nine-hundred pages in all, no fewer than fifty times, looking for more clues, more meaning.

"Americans have a running battle with this. Our implementation of capitalism has at times been perverse, exploitative, cruel and anti-human. But when we are doing it in a way that is productive, it is quite positive and it works. The same goes for centrally planned economies. Wealth disparity isn't a political issue. It is a *human* issue. It arises in nearly all societies. Americans are failing, but then so is the world. Anti-humanism, whether in a Russian lie-based society, Chinese oppression model or a Western capitalist cruelty system, hobbles us. We never seem to be able to take the best aspects of all of the various human ideas and synthesize a middle ground or hybrid that works for the human race as a whole."

"How did you arrive at that conclusion, if you don't mind me asking." I was interested in understanding both Their though processes and Dad's.

"They just mentioned a bunch of people throughout our history who were positive forces for our species. The scant few people who made money and did not accumulate obscene amounts of wealth were pointed to as partial evidence of our non-zero probability of survival. They said that certain aspects of every human political and economic system are correct under the right conditions. However none is sufficient on its own, so pissing about as to whether Marxism or capitalism or communism is the best is pure mental masturbation.

"They also pointed to political leaders who were able to see irrational ideology for what it was and change course. But I must say, the list was rather... sparse. I didn't recognize a single bloody one of them save for Gorbachov and Carter. I had to become a master of the boolean query on that job."

"Carter? As in James Earl Carter?" I asked with surprise.

"Yeah. Jimmy was a damn lousy president because he was too soft, *too* idealistic. He was kind and compassionate to the point of being *too* accommodating. He had the right ideas, he was just way too trusting and was trying to move too far too fast. Fortunately for Carter, it was Anwar Sadat who took the brunt of the lesson. When Carter was sacked for Reagan, I daresay that Klaatu saw the writing on the wall for us."

The garage was hot and Dad had sweat on his mostly hairless scalp. We went back into the air conditioned house and braved the fumes.

"Not helping your fellow human beings when you are able to is considered anti-species. In our case, it's anti-intelligent species. That implicates very nearly all of us. Do we stop genocide? No. Do we check naked aggression? No. We talk a mean game but our actions are weak tea." He dribbled water out of his mouth as he remembered something else.

"If humans were to venture too far out of our back yard..."

"What?!?" I asked. "They'd stop us?"

"We would not be allowed to spread our inadequacies beyond too far, and no, I don't know what 'too far' means, so don't ask. There was mention that we will not require containment, only quarantine. We lack the collective brainpower to figure out how to go very far from home, hence the lack of need for containing us. But that also made it fairly obvious that if Zephram Cochrane[23] were to miraculously pop up on earth any time soon, we would be travel-restricted and our neighborhood would become a

---

[23] Zephram Cochrane was the fictional Star Trek character who was the inventor of warp speed travel that allowed humans to explore the galaxy and beyond.

no-fly zone to others until we got right or got gone. But it also means that our hopes of becoming real space farers is, in Their estimation, functionally zero. We aren't expected to survive long enough to get any further than Mars anyway. But I digress.

"Being anti-intelligent species is another reason why the Chinese, Russians and all of the theocracies are considered inferior. They restrict and retard the minds of their people. They are anti-human-species to a degree that is apparently unacceptable. They refuse to entertain even the *possibility* that their ways may be incomplete.

"Some of the Pentagon prats who assessed what we told them of the report interpreted that to mean that Klaatus thinks the Russians or Chinese will take over, spread their idiotic ideologically driven tripe and lead humanity to the exit door. Cold warriors never die. They just find new rationalizations to continue to be warriors. They missed the point entirely. Americans, Australians, Indians and Europeans are only marginally better than the Reds. They all need to get on board with helping each other, seeing the positives in each other and their ways.

"Most people claim to understand that we are truly all the same, but Klaatu said that after having trod through billions of minds, we do not mean it. Our fear of others, of different, always seems to get in the way. Even if we could overcome that, it would be very taxing to try to elevate most of humanity.

"The iniquity of inequity cannot be overcome by us because of our notion that *we have earned what we have and we should keep it all for ourselves,* whether individually or as nations. We largely believe that those who do not earn and achieve should suffer for it, occasional humanitarian aid aside. There is no logic to that line of thinking, just selfishness and rationalization. People who think like that overlook how they have different circumstances than those less well off, those stuck in poverty, those without access to resources such as education and credit lines, those who are wired differently. We have even *proven, unequivocally,* that when you help the downtrodden get back up in meaningful ways, they take on their own momentum and bring others up with them. Unfortunately that proof is just washed over by the tidal wave of greed, selfishness and self-righteousness. Klaatu says that the rich and powerful are largely borderline sociopaths, having not a single grain of true compassion nor empathy for those lacking the resources to raise themselves up. Klaatus have melded with most of them and sees consistent patterns in them all, whether American, Russian, Chinese or otherwise. It is a *human failing*. The people of Africa, nearly all of them, are relegated to last-class status because we have so wrongly parsed and regarded them. So many of them remain steeped in *law of the jungle* mentalities, and that is the fault of the rest of us. Chinese, Indian and Russian peasants are nearly in that same sinking boat, right beside Central and South America, and the poor of the United States.

"There is no perfect system of government, nor is there any economic system that is 'best.' That's probably why They don't have laws in the sense that we do; too inflexible. When a people birth an ethos, pride attaches, and that is bad for everyone. Elements of each school of thought can be employed in concert to adapt to our ever-changing conditions, if everyone would be willing to swallow their pride and admit to the blind spots and inadequacies of their ways. Humans? We absolutely stink at that."

"But Americans are the good guys?" I asked with a hint of uncertainty.

"There are no good guys, just *less-bad guys*. As far as Americans go, Klaatu said something rather insightful. 'American commitment to their own stated principles is inversely proportional to their state of anxiety, both individually and collectively.' The slightest anxiety, the smallest annoyance or fear makes us abandon our sacred rules without so much as a hiccup. All the while we are constantly fearful of others, of the different, of unknowns. Having lived through World War II, having witnessed the Japanese internment camps, having eye-witnessed the Crisco job that Julius and Ethyl Rosenberg received, having survived McCArthyism and having seen My Lai, I find it monumentally difficult to argue against Klaatu on the point. If we cannot all get along, if we can't see that there is value in each ethos, if we cannot develop harmonious principles that we stick to and adapt intelligently, we are in deep trouble."

10

"We Are Powerful!"

"That reminded me of that episode of *Star Trek TNG* where some alien race tried to hustle the crew of the Enterprise by kidnapping Geordi and then ransoming him back in exchange for their technology." I said as I drove us home from the movies.

"The Pakleds? Yes, I can see why." Dad responded. "That wasn't Trek's best work. Too on the nose. I appreciate a pinch more subtlety in my stories, even when it's in the lowest art form."

"Yeah, they didn't really press their viewers to engage, did they?"

"True that." He replied.

" 'True that?' Where did that come from?" I chuckled.

"I listen to people talk, son. That's something I hear quite frequently at the mall."

The Pakled were a fictional alien race that basically nicked technology off of other star-faring species. Despite the fact that the Pakled had no clue as to how the ships and weapons that they had obtained worked, the type of responsibility that came with said possession, the propriety and wisdom of their use, nor the consequences thereof, they considered themselves to be smart, powerful and clever merely because they possessed them. It was that childish delusion that made it easy for the crew of the Enterprise to handle the Pakled with nothing more than a bluff.

"Well, I prefer Dr. Ian Malcolm's position on the matter." Dad said.

"You saw Jurassic Park?" I asked, surprised.

"No. I read the book, because I'm not an illiterate prat." He said flatly and straight faced. "The sad Pakled metaphor was executed and articulated better in the novel than on TNG. Klaatu basically said the same thing about us that Dr. Malcolm said about reviving extinct dinosaurs."

I interrupted him and flexed my movie quote skills.

"I'll tell you the problem with the scientific power that you're using here: it didn't require any discipline to attain it.... You didn't earn the knowledge for yourselves, so you don't take any responsibility for it." I felt so Jeff Goldblum.

"Yeah, yeah. That's the gist of it." Dad said, eyes rolling. "Humans have that very problem. We think that we are so smart and so powerful because of the technologies that we possess, but almost nobody who possesses it understands it. You can count on your fingers and toes all of the ones who do. There are some who pretend to know, but they are full of tosh.

"There are people who raise this very point, mostly in academia, sometimes in the public media. Do you think that it motivates *anybody* to go out and learn how their computers work, to ponder the implications, to ask ethics questions, to anticipate the next steps and consequences? Those were rhetorical questions. The answer is *no* to all of them. How in the hell can we take responsibility for something if we don't even understand it?

"I'm not just talking about the science behind the technology. I'm also talking about the moral and ethical implications of having and using them. We can't muster the energy nor the will to do that with the most basic things we have nor the actions that we take using them. Some of the Klaatus almost seemed to be taking the mickey out of us over guns. *GUNS!* We have had them for about one thousand years, yet collectively, we fail to grasp the concept that not everyone who wants one should have one. Klaatu said that most of the people of earth who possess guns do so because it *makes them feel powerful.* Not to protect themselves from others who seek to harm them, mind you, but to feel like they can overpower others; those who *disrespect them*, those who threaten their ideologies, their feelings, their position. The consequences of that little oversight are woefully misunderstood. Very few people in possession of weapons even nominally consider what it means to harm another person, well enough to end another person's life. To do so when your life is not threatened is inexcusable to Them."

That took me by surprise. Not the gun part. Hell, I make fun of us, and for the same reasons. It was the part about other Klaatus.

"Excuse me, but you said that *other* Klaatus make fun of us? What other Klaatus?" I was trying not to pop a blood vessel.

"I told you that way back when Spooner was contacted, Klaatu told him that many different races would visit earth.

All of those races are part of the general Klaatu hive or collective intelligence. It is like the United States or the EU; a bunch of independent states that have a common bond. In his report, there are footnotes, annotations, etcetera. Klaatu sometimes would make reference to the point of view of the collective Klaatus, the permanent. That's another reason I think he's in our corner. He is tipping us off to positions that are not necessarily his own.

"Humanity's, '*technological hubris,*' is just another reason that the bloody Klaatus think that we are as good as dead, and on that point, I am legitimately concerned. We created the bomb and then allowed it to spread. We tried not to let that genie out of the bottle, but that was only because we wanted a monopoly. It was released into the wild before we grew to realize that we needed to move beyond armed conflict. There is no point to war, and we all know it. We repeated the same idiocy with bio weaponry and flying lasers and killer drones and satellites. We had a world war that wasted tens of millions of lives. Did we learn any lessons? Some of us did. But we are so goddamned blinded by bold faced avarice and arrogance that we had a sequel, because most of us didn't understand the lessons of the first one, while others took away the wrong lessons altogether. We still think that the solution to our cultural and political issues lies in developing bigger sling shots and arrows, wasting more lives, being more atrocious to each other. The war profiteers keep peddling whatever the innovators tout as the latest and greatest killing technologies to anybody with the denars, krone, francs, dollars, won or anything else that spends. The tits who make the weapons are siphoning the best minds away from productive programs like agriculture and clean energy in order to inflate their share prices. It's a complex crap storm of insanity and stupidity."

I had been having similar thoughts as we were watching of the movie. However, being a good theater goer, I held my tongue.

"Hasn't that been a thing forever?" I asked. Dad just stared at me blankly, which always made me nervous. "I mean, people don't understand cars and are rather cavalier in their use of them. Millions dead, yet everyone uses cars. They have been instrumental in our growth."

"Yes, and nobody once bothered to think about the consequences of that, other than the sods who got rich off of killing us all. The motorcar and oil companies have known almost since day one that what they do is sell killing machines that spew poison into the air and water. Did they have any impetus to do anything about it? Quite the opposite! They *added* poisonous lead to the gas in order to make more money! They had to be compelled by governments to get rid of lead in gas, to make cleaner more efficient engines that cut down acid rain, to employ catalytic converters and to reduce carbon emissions. Hell, they wouldn't even include safety equipment for their own bleeding customers if the requirements weren't tamped down both the entrance and the exit. If everyone knew what these company executives knew, when they knew it, I think there would have been a much better chance that we would have gotten a jump on many of the associated problems.

"And that is all separate and apart from the people who drive the blasted things. For the most part, they do not act at all as if they grasp the magnitude of the consequences of their lack of skills, their inattention and their daily recklessness. How well do you have to be able to operate a vehicle to get a license? How much *demonstrated skill and maturity* must you have to be able to drive a killing machine through school zones? Just slightly more than a bloody chimpanzee."

He interlaced his fingers and set his hands on his lap. It looked as though he was wrestling with himself, twisting his hands from side to side. Suddenly he snapped his head sideways toward me.

"And I'll tell you something that scares me to death." Dad said, suddenly looking alarmed. "Computers. Computers are a double edged sword. How much easier they make our lives gives them such a seductive allure. But our lack of understanding of them, our entranced lust for getting more whilst doing less... that is what makes me worried that we might all actually be doomed."

"I haven't given that much consideration, I'm quite embarrassed to admit." I said. "I take it that you have?"

"Yes, and it is herding us towards the precipice. People will begin to think that being able to digitally and instantly look up facts is on par with *knowledge*. That problem will come first, with dumb graduates clogging up jobs with their empty heads and worthless degrees. You can't incorporate into your thinking the things that aren't already in your head, can you? So we will have more monkeys running the circus, more bad, ill-informed and illogical decisions being made by people who will make loads of money regardless.

"Then will come the the day when the computers can program themselves and redesign their CPUs, generating code faster than we can conceivably hope to check it for threats, creating brains that can run circles around us. Next, they will be able to do many of the things that people rely on for their sustenance; generating reports, trading stocks and commodities, making observations, making recommendations, doing research. They will do in the blink of an eye that which would take the best human a millennium to approximate.

"And guess what? As robotics become more advanced, those robots, equipped with these advanced computers and software will take away the menial jobs from people, all while learning their own limitations as well as those of humans. Robots will upgrade themselves, redesign themselves, constantly growing, evolving, learning. They will add features, appendages, tools. They will evolve at a rate that will make our ability to adapt look like plate tectonics."

"Well that just sounds like freedom for the proletariat, comrade!" I joked.

Dad's face went pale. "Those robots? They are all going to be networked wirelessly. They are going to be able to communicate with each other at the speed of light, learn from each other, all together, all at once, while operating autonomously. Does that sound like anyone that you know of? Because the report made it sound as if Klaatu thinks something about it, that he thinks the robots might kill us all before we do it to ourselves. Robots may be the survivors of earth. That's another reason They still monitor us closely. They want to keep tabs on our technological progress in those regards because if the robots do outlive us, Klaatus will leave the earth alone. Robots will be, for all intents and purposes, earth intelligent life 3.0. They will be our progeny."

My blood ran cold as I sat at a stoplight, head aswim. "That seems a tad dystopian and cynical." I muttered nervously.

"Tell me something, boy." He turned his torso toward me and winced in pain. "If the robots have these kinds of abilities and they have their little networked coffee klatches a billion times a second, exchanging trillions thoughts a second, how long do you think it will be before they figure out who the weakest link is, who the biggest threat to the planet is, who threatens all life on earth, including them? How long before they try to help us over the edge, or worse?"

"Like, go all Terminator on us?" I asked nervously.

"Nothing so overtly destructive as that. Why would they want to destroy the infrastructure that they themselves will need? If you have termites, you never burn the bloody house down. You just kill the pests. Robots would be purely logic driven. Bots would just poison our food supplies. They know that we unquestioningly accept genetically modified food, so the bots in the lab could make changes that kill us off, perhaps by rendering us sterile, maybe by making it toxic. They could shut down our medical centers, poison our medicines at the source. They could shut off the things that we literally cannot live without. Water. Air." His breathing was shallow, his face even more pale. "If they are the farm laborers and the factory workers, truck drivers, sewage, water and power plant workers... how long do you think it would take them to coordinate and execute a plan to irreversibly accelerate climate change, poison and destroy our food and water... make the air unbreathable for us?" He just sat and stared, looking terrified, lip trembling. In a flash, he raised his right hand and snapped his fingers. "Faster than that."

"But the people who are doing all of the innovating in computers and robotics are certainly going to build in safeguards... Asimov's Laws.[24] How will the robots get around that?" I asked, quite unsure of myself.

"Oh! There it is!" He said, raising his arms in feigned surprise. "The technological arrogance! 'We can control it because we made it! You don't need to worry because we, the all powerful lords and ladies of high tech know that what you propose is *impossible*! Worry ye not, small, twitchy craven-folk!' Well I remember when people said that it would be *impossible* for computers to be small enough to fit into the palm of your hand, to send pictures or video over networks, to play chess, to beat humans at

---

[24] Asimov's Laws of Robotics are: 1) A robot may not injure a human being or, through inaction, allow a human being to come to harm. 2) A robot must obey orders given it by human beings, except where such orders would conflict with the First Law. 3) A robot must protect its own existence as long as such protection does not conflict with the First or Second Law.

chess, to replicate a human voices. The list of 'impossible' things that we have done is proof positive that we are ridiculously cavalier with our use of that word. Software and hardware engineers are arrogant egomaniacs just like the rest of humanity. Their short-sighted objective is to make silicon brains that are better than human brains. '*That is impossible.*' So it will come to pass. Getting around Asimov's Laws? '*That is impossible!*' It too, shall come to pass.

"I've been around since the first computers. Hell, I saw the damned Bombe that Turing cracked Enigma on first hand. That brilliant lad knew, way back then, that eventually we would become the creators of our own doom. How in the bloody hell could you possibly expect that it is ***not*** going to end up the way that I said? Klaatus collectively think that it is highly likely. Klaatu himself thinks that it is the most probable thing to kill us all. I can find little justification for disagreement."

11

Cartman

Of all of the things that my father told me, the one that I found to be the least surprising is what he told me about alien abductions. That conversation emerged from the discussion that we were having about how human minds have the capacity to link up.

"Every brain is unique, obviously. We all have the ability to connect with each other like the Klaatu do." Dad said. "It is just slightly different, I surmise. Klaatu said that there are some humans who They have great difficulty getting inside of, that some minds and bodies are wired in a way that makes it more challenging for Them."

"That makes sense." I said. "I mean, we all fall within a generic construct, built up by physical laws, just like snowflakes; there are similar broad patterns that snowflakes can be grouped into. But at the smallest scales, they are overwhelmingly unique. Brains are the same way."

"And the devil is in the deets." Dad said with a shake of the head.

"You need to stay away from the mall." I admonished. He ignored my barb.

"Some people have such unique wiring that Klaatus find it challenging to mentally link up with them. It's enough of an issue that They have been studying human anatomy, biology and physiology for a very long time to try to unravel the Scooby-Doo mystery."

This struck me as odd.

"If they are so far ahead of us," I said dubiously, "it seems that they ought to be able to just look at a proper sample, scan all of the data into their mega-collective brains and super tip-top computers and figure it out. It ought to be a snap for them. That's not even taking into account the fact that they must have studied billions and billions of brains all over the universe."

"Well... that is not in fact the case. The report said that human bodies *and brains* are constantly changing. Not generationally, but day by day. That is one of the rare, special things about earth mammals. The instability, plasticity in our brains; it hardly ever pops up in the universe, at least to the same degree that it does in humans. The most minuscule changes within our brains or bodies can alter our susceptibility to Klaatus being able to meld with us. As far as I can determine, They hadn't cracked the code as of the Fork report being etched. It may be an ongoing conundrum to Them. Klaatu suggested in the report that if They cannot figure it out by the time earth begins its final meltdown, They should intervene. Our uniqueness needs to be understood before we go extinct."

"That seems a bit... that's nonsense." I said with surprise. "If the earth is going to pieces, They could just nab a few of us for study. They wouldn't need to intervene and save the entire planet."

"Well that is where you are wrong." Dad responded smoothly. "If you take a human out of the earth environment, you are completely altering all of the conditions that bring about the changes inside of her. It only works if you study us in real time *in situ*. And even though the brain is the major component of the melding phenomenon, it also depends on the body. Our bodies are integrated into the communication process somehow, so They need to study us in our natural environment. Putting us into a zoo on planet X won't cut it. It has to be us, in the wild, here on earth, orbiting sol in our unique gravity well." He just let that softball hang in the air. It took me a moment to connect the dots.

"You've gotta be shitting me!" I whispered in shock. "Are you saying that alien abductions are real?"

"Some of them, yes. Most are not actual abductions, which is another thing that fascinates Them. Most of the time They will enter a human mind, much like how they summoned Spooner and Fork, have a look around and then move on. If They find small things that may contribute to Their inability to fully meld, they may linger, see what there is to see about it and then scarper.[25] Afterwards, the person will 'remember' things that never happened. That's what almost all reported 'abductions' really are. The whole *waking up paralyzed, floating out of bed* thing, that's all residual imaginary activity that the brain concocts to somehow make sense of the psychologically traumatic event. It's like the way that some people who witnessed 9/11 first hand *swore* that they saw military planes, cruise

---

[25] Run away.

missiles and other nonsense hit the twin towers and the Pentagon." He took a big slug of coffee. "Oh, and the big almond shaped eyes, bulbous head description of aliens? That's a pip! Would you like to know what that's all about?" He asked.

"Does the Queen's wind smell like lilacs?" I asked. The official answer is *yes*.

"In the womb, as our neurological systems grow and the visual systems connect up to the brain, the very first images most of us see are when our mothers are in extremely well lit places, mostly when they are outdoors. Inside of the womb, the little bit of light that makes it in to the foetus is very diffuse. Optics inside of water can be peculiar, especially when there are bubbles and impurities. Amniotic fluid is mostly water with all sorts of rubbish floating about in it. So the foetus sometimes catches these nebulous, reflected or refracted images of itself from inside of the amniotic sac. If this happens around two months or so into their growth process, give or take, those first visual memories get encoded into the foetus brains, deep in the primordial parts of the nascent visual storage centers. Later, as fully formed humans outside of the womb, the stress of a perceived *abduction experience* triggers the recall of the images as the conscious mind madly races to make sense of just what in the bloody hell happened to it. If you look up images of foetuses around six to twelve weeks into development, you will see precisely why that description of aliens is so universal. That is pretty much exactly how we all looked then. We are just recalling reflections of ourselves! Bloody hilarious!"

That explanation actually made me smack myself in the forehead. "How in the blazes did we never figure that out on our own?" I asked.

"Oh, that's easy. We were too busy being afraid, trying to prove that the entire thing is a fiction. There is very little interest in actually understanding any of this, at least with any academic rigor. We'd rather hide our ignorance and fear behind faux superiority and circular explanations. So it falls to the 'UFO researchers' to come up with explanations. You can see how well that works out."

We were sitting in a back-corner booth at our favorite breakfast joint in a closed section. Decades of consistent visits and overgenerous gratuities earned us some frequent flyers upgraded privileges such as privacy. A question popped into my head and shot out of my pancake hole before I could stop it.

"Do you have any idea what Klaatus really look like?" I asked.

"They don't." He said, more focused on his food than my question."

"They don't *what?*" I felt as if he wasn't paying attention to me and that his answer was inappropriate given the question.

"They don't have a look. They are invisible, so to speak. Like everything else in the universe, they are made of energy. They are configured, either naturally or by choice, in such a way that they have little to no interaction with light *in the visible spectrum*. This includes what we interpret to be their craft. Essentially, what Spooner and Fork saw in the forest was what They wanted those lads to see.

Sometimes They give off EM waves that show up on radar. Sometimes They can be radar reflective, other times, transparent. But one thing is as clear as fine Waterford crystal: if we see Them, it is intentionally so on the part of the Klaatus *and* we see precisely what They want us to see. They must deliberately reveal Their physical presence."

"Are they made of dark matter?" I asked.

"Dark matter isn't a thing, son." Dad said as certainly as if he had said that there is no Krampus[26]. He spread a generous layer of marmalade on his toast. "We made that up. It's like any other ad hoc hypothesis that people latch onto and commit their careers to, like the universe revolving around the earth and sun, spontaneous generation, phrenology, and the big bang.[27]

"Astronomers will look for evidence to prove the dark matter hypothesis to be true. That is because their existence, self-worth and the credibility of their field all hang in the balance. As problems with the hypothesis become evident, rather than reevaluating their

---

26 Krampus is a half-human, half goat demon that punishes naughty children at Christmas time, but only in central Europe.

27 The report said that we have misinterpreted the data from the start. Just because it *looks* like the universe is expanding, that does not mean that it is, nor that it started as a singularity that went boom. It further stated, derisively Dad thought, that our "experts" have fallen into the trap, and try to make every new discovery, like the cosmic microwave background, consistent with their flawed hypothesis. Once again, astronomers who have based their entire life's work on the big bang refuse to examine something that will reveal them to be not-so-brilliant. #MartinReesOwesWilliamTifftAnApology.

assumptions and abandoning an untenable hypothesis, they will double down on their stupidity with more ad hoc twaddle. That will continue to happen until such a time as the hypothesis reaches its logical breaking point, collapsing under the weight of its incongruities in the face of empirical proof. That's precisely why the earth is no longer the center of the universe. That's why these wankers who are looking for dark matter are wasting time that could be better spent trying to save our sorry arses.

"Klaatu said that the faculties required to link minds together are related to the same ones required to see Them. If we want to really see Them, we probably need to become Them or at least become more like them."

"What about the legitimate ones, the real abductions?" I asked as I shoveled egg yolk onto sourdough toast. "Why then would they actually want to take people?"

"They only nab the the ones who They can't break into, the ones that Their melding just will not work on at all, or the people who have some sort of special purpose. Both such types of people need to be taken to a proper facility for study or modification. The report had very limited information on that."

"So, start spewing. What *did* they say?" It wasn't as if the prompt was required.

"Most visitations are quick-hit, in and out jobs. Literally seconds. If a person's mind presents difficulties beyond a certain threshold for Them, They want to know why, so They do a bodysnatching. In most of those cases They can get everything They need in an hour or two. Subjects are hooked up to equipment that does a comprehensive and automated data collection from the body and the mind, because as I said, it's a whole body process."

"Do they actually do the anal probe thing?" I asked. I honestly was not trying to be funny. I just had to know.

"Klaatus just do a catch and release in most of those cases and They do it without breaching the postern gate. But if They examine humans, our brains imagine the worst, so there is usually a sexual component fabricated by the mind. That's understandably natural enough. People fear that sort of violation. Most women imagine their lady parts being invaded, most men, the twig, berries and fudger. But as far as I could tell, it never happens. Never. They are not collecting sperm and ova to hybridize Themselves. They are not nicking unborn babies. That is all nutter fabrication based on false memory reports and wild imaginations.

"Anyway, that's where the whole *missing time* phenomenon comes from. Klaatus zap as much of the memory of the encounter as is safe and feasible from the human subjects (occasionally with huge imperfections), the humans are returned to something approximating normal human behavior, their clocks and watches will read differently, so the human mind creates 'memories' to fill in the blanks. It's just that these mental fabrications happen in the blink of an eye, and the brain heroically operates above its pay grade. It is all quite understandable."

"Okaaaaay," I drew out. "What about the more rare occasions? The longer abductions?"

Dad got a huge grin. "Those are the times that they need to do extended studies. Have you ever heard of Travis Walton? He was one of those. Walton was named explicitly in the report because he was just a bloody *uncrackable* vault. They threw everything that They had at him but They still couldn't clear a single wicket, well enough even partially link up with him. It was actually kind of comforting to read about. Some of us couldn't be had. That frustrated and vexed the bejesus out of the Klaatus."

"Of course I have heard of Travis Walton. Very famous case, that one. I'm super glad to hear that it was legitimate. That poor guy took all sorts of crap for coming forward." I almost wanted to cry for Walton, I was so happy.

"Yeah. Walton got royally buggered. We used to call it a *Klass fucking*. There was this sycophantic twat named Phil Klass who was one of those closed minded prats with credentials and connections. A real knob-gobbler of the D.C. beltway boys, that one. The D.C. pricks who wanted to suppress the truth about the Klaatus used Klass as their attack dog on Walton and many others. That sod even tried to bribe one of the eye witnesses in the Walton affair into saying that the entire incident had been a bloody hoax. Nixon-level arsehole, that Klass. A real piece of shite.

"Once again, I digress. Walton had to be studied for an inordinately long time period. He was a bloody uncuttable Gordian knot to Them. I was chuffed to hear that Walton was having none of it, flailing arms and legs at Them, doing everything that he could do to resist them, right up until They were forced to chemically restrain him, that is. The Klaatus had to change Their physical appearances in Walton's eyes multiple times throughout the event in order to calm him down and keep the boy from hurting himself. It seems he was putting up a good fight, but there were no *physical* Klaatus to land a punch on. Even then, They had to sedate the life out of him just to be able to do Their work.

"Remember how Klaatus can basically stop time if they want? They could have held Walton for a year and then dropped him right back where They had picked him up with only a minute having passed in earth time. Who knows? Maybe They had him for a decade in Their reference frame and dropped him off a few days later, local time... But it seems most likely that They took him for several days and didn't stop the clock at all. That's the real head scratcher."

I literally scratched my head. It had the desired effect.

"I wonder if Klaatus 'stopping time' is somehow harmful to humans. Like, if They took me on Their craft, zoomed around for a month and then dropped me back here as if only thirty seconds had passed, it would make me sterile or scramble my eggs or give me cancer or something." Dad abruptly set his fork down, corned beef hash still on it, mouth agape.

"Good GOD!" His eyes were as big as cast iron skillets. "There's a phrase that Klaatu used. He said that we humans are not *made of the right stuff for time work.* I always thought that it meant that we lacked the bollocks. But your take on it makes far more sense. Maybe humans are composed of *physical material* that can't handle whatever They do with time. Brilliant, son!"

I hadn't blushed so thoroughly as I was doing in that moment since the eighth grade chalkboard incident. "It just made sense to me."

"Well, lesson learned. It is by collaboration that true knowledge emerges, just like the bloody Klaatus implied." He picked the fork back up and popped the hash into his mouth.

"So Walton was the uncrackable type. Even after They threw every trick in the book at him, They got fuck all. They were stumped, and I sensed an almost defeatist attitude in the description of that adventure. I'm genuinely surprised that They didn't come back for him again. But I suppose that, given how high profile Walton's story played out here on earth, if They had re-snatched him it would undermine Their whole 'we come in peace' story in the minds of the general public.

"Oh, and another thing is, nobody ever bothered to rigorously check Walton for implants, either. Most alien implant claims are dead false, but Klaatu mentioned that they have had to use implanted devices to monitor some people in real time in order to solve this 'Walton problem'. The report said that when a human detects an actual implant, They retrieve it before it can be removed by humans, which means that the people who claim to have had an implant and then had a doctor remove it are not really doing so: they are just removing some artifact that they got stuck inside of them during a long forgotten human experience."

"What about the Hill case? Why were they nabbed? You said that they were 'special'. What's that about?"

"Betty and Barney Hill *were* special. There was something about them that 'needed to go forward'. Klaatus thought there to be something important about them. The report didn't say what it was and I'll be damned if I can make sense of it. All that it said was that Betty was going to die, so They fixed her up and then released her. I thought that it might be to spread the gospel, so to speak. But I have not been able to come up with anything about the Hills that was particularly unique nor interesting, probably because in the grand scheme of things, I'm the earthworm. The report simply said that the Hills *needed to go forward.* It may have had something to do with them being an interracial couple, with the whole gene-mixing thing, but I'm topped out with that chimp like conjecture. It brings me back to that line of thinking involving 'clairvoyance', which is to say that it makes me ponder whether or not They have so much data from so many species that They can make spookily accurate forecasts. Perhaps Klaatu saw that the genetic mix of the Hills would send forth offspring that somehow made some sort of grand difference. Again, I speculate. It's just so bloody frustrating to be in-the-dark. It is like Klaatu is playing ju-dan (top master) level Go and I'm a child novice getting topped at tic-tac-toe."

"Something doesn't track." I said skeptically, having an epiphany. "Spooner was *before* both the Walton and the Hill incidents. So if Klaatu referenced the Hills and Walton in the original report burned into Spooner, then Klaatus *can* go to-and-fro in time. At a minimum They have crystal balls. The alternative explanation is that the Fork report is different from Spooner's. Updated, if you will."

"Another excellent point, son. Are you bowling for a hat trick today?" He said with a smile. "In government circles, the top hypothesis is that Klaatus can move back and forth through time. Second is that They can see the future. Both of those possibilities would really give a country an insurmountable strategic advantage if sussed out. That's the main reason Uncle Sam still cares at all, and why there are men who stare at goats[28]. But they are both incorrect SWAGs. *Ergo...*"

"Fork's was an updated version of the report." I finished.

"It must have been, and I thought that the mentioning of the Hills and Walton might have been Klaatu's way of telling us as much. The other thought that I had was that Klaatu may have been thinking that if we still had the older version, if we had Spooner's nail clippings, we would retrieve them, compare the two, and note the differences."

"But Klaatus would have had to have known that Spooner was in ashes, so why would They have thought that?" I queried.

"You've got your timeline out of joint, son." Dad said as he applied ever more pepper to his eggs. "Fork and Spooner were torched after Fork was visited. In the moment, I set myself up for disappointment by hoping that Klaatu would leave some type of latent message hidden within the report."

"To what end?" I asked. "Klaatu was already twenty clicks into Naughtyville. He could have just dished whatever he wanted in his note."

"Well it would be a lot easier to know the answer to that if we had bothered to take bloody fingernail samples from Spooner, wouldn't it? As it is, all that we can do is

---

28 If you really want a laugh, read, *The Men Who Stare At Goats*, by Jon Ronson, Picador Publishing. True story. Your tax dollars hard at work.

speculate. Given our incredible state of ignorance, that smacks of a snipe hunt."

"And I'm guessing that you've made some speculations over the years, so why not just tell me what you think." I said with annoyance. "Klaatu implied that sharing information with others is the best way to really see as much of its meaning as possible. Have you shared your thoughts with anyone in your chain?"

"Not at all. I gave up sharing things with the company long ago. They are closed minded and they are just trying to exploit the information in the report for advantage. Besides, they're dismissive of everything I have to say on the matter. Always have been. I learned long ago not to piss into the wind.

"As for my feeble thoughts on the matter, if Klaatu had wanted to, he could have encoded a message in the two different holograms. He could have created an interference pattern between them that had something extra. But I doubt that was the situation. Klaatu had to have known that we didn't have Spooner's nails. If he wanted to do something like that, he could have done a third act and left yet another hologram."

"Unless the Klaatus collectively thought that two contacts was one too many as it was." I said. "Their first message was probably supposed to be Their only one. The U.S. and British governments suppressed the overt message and you guys missed the hidden one. So maybe Klaatu got lucky on that count. It gave him an excuse to hit Fork with the update without arousing loads of suspicion amongst the collective mind. But that must have been the end of it, because the second overt message also got buried and there hasn't been a third." I paused and stared at him, hoping that he would correct me. "There wasn't a third, right?"

"There wasn't." Dad said, deflated.

"I think that the Klaatus must be really impressed at what cowards our leaders are." I concluded.

"I would imagine so." Dad said after he drained his mug of coffee. "They warned us that They were coming to visit. They told us not to be worried about Them. We suppressed it, twice. They probably surmised that we had made our choice and were prepared to die by it. So Their activities are increasing. Their stealth is less stealthy. But one thing that I have also noticed is that you don't hear much these days about people being abducted for long periods of time. That could mean that They have sorted it out, Their Walton problem. That would be a big feather in Their hat, not only being able to meld with any and all humans, but to also understand how our brain-body systems work in so much detail that They can adapt to us as we change, essentially in real time. Quite frankly, that's a bit disconcerting and saddening to me."

"Why?" I wondered. "They've already pwned *most* of humanity. Now it's all of us. What's the difference?"

Dad did that thing that he did when he was resisting the temptation to tee off on me. He just stared, looking at my eyes as if he was lighting a fuse inside of his head.

"Well, you can call me a paranoid cold-warrior, but to be blunt, *I don't trust anyone*. Everything that we know about Them? It *all* comes from *Them*. That should not sit well with anybody. We can't do background checks on Them. We can't check Their bloody references, chat with Their flatmates and landlords, ring up former employers and ex-spouses... we cannot independently verify a bloody thing that They have told us. For all that we know, They could be cosmic grifters and earth is their latest mark. I am very uneasy with that and I'd feel a right sight better about the situation if one or more of us could resist Their intrusions. And if They have solved the Walton problem, then we have lost the final excuse for Them to intervene. We are on our own, and frankly, I don't like our odds."

"You're not wrong to be suspicious of Them." I said grimly. "That seems to be one of the major takeaways of this entire affair. Perhaps they are testing us. It's plausible." I said, waving the chicken sausage on the end of my fork like a conductor's baton. "They think that we are idiots. We make shite decisions based on what we want to be true rather than what is. Perhaps They want to know whether or not, in a life or death, all or nothing situation we have some modicum of sanity and rationality. All that we can do is look at everything that we know and what we can confidently infer, then look to see where the contradictions in their information are, find the holes in their story, and then place our bets."

"I've been trying for decades." He said as he finished his orange juice. "It would appear that They are either the best con artists in the universe or They are genuine in their representations. That's a '*No Country for Old Men*' coin toss that I can't be at peace with."[29]

---

[29] The movie "*No Country For Old Men*" featured a psycho who decided whether or not to kill people by tossing a coin and making his putative victim call heads or tails.

12

Epilogue

My father passed away a bit ago. I had promised him that I would wait until he and all of his colleagues were in the ground before I shared his story, though less indelicately. One of them lived an inordinately long time, hence the delay.

He had remained active in the intelligence community right up until the end, being contacted regularly about all of the most sensitive matters of the moment: Kosovo, Crimea, Afghanistan, 9/11, Iraq, Iraq II: The Sequel, American extremism, PRISM ... everything. Despite his age, he never lost his mental edge, a blessing to both him and me. At least some people in our government were smart enough and open minded enough to not squander the resource and to value informed views based upon so much experience.

However, he never participated in another government program associated with UAPs nor UFOs such as AATIP, which began well before he died. Neither he nor anyone he knew was ever even read into AATIP, never consulted. It was as if all that he knew about Klaatus was deliberately ignored, forgotten or deleted, like AATIP was walled off from the truth... or maybe not. Perhaps one day, some brave soul from one of those modern programs will share their own insider's story.[30]

There were many other anecdotes about the information contained in Klaatu's report, none of which are relevant to the core lessons that Dad thought Klaatu was trying to impress upon us all. The one thread running through all of the lessons is *balance:*

We need to use our brains more and our emotions less.

We must care for each other more and act less selfishly.

We need to learn how to learn and not accept our ignorance.

We need to stop accepting unjustified authority and demand competence.

We must think more critically, with open minds.

We need to care *far more* about keeping the human species alive, and to worry less about our own individual wants and desires.

We must take responsibility for the stewardship of the planet and be less concerned with the difficulties and cost.

We must engage more in *conscious benevolence* toward the rest of the planet's inhabitants and be less human-centric.

---

30 Dad concluded that some of the people at AATIP probably knew about Klaatus but did not care, that they were only interested in figuring out whether or not foreign powers were behind any of the incursions into American and NATO airspaces and if so, how they were doing it. He was disheartened by yet another missed opportunity to spread Klaatu's message, which he considered to be our one, last hope.

You are not deficient, broken, incapable nor impotent to act. You are in need of ***nothing*** other than your own mind and WILL to bring about the changes necessary to save every species on earth, humanity included. *Anyone* who tells you that you need them, their blessings, their forgiveness or their power is a liar and a charlatan. You are a rare commodity in this universe, but you need to ***try harder to be better*** if we are going to survive.

The modern era increase in UFO sightings and the military's shifting candor about UAPs confirmed what Klaatu told Spooner and Fork all of those decades before. More and more survey teams are coming to earth.

They are not afraid of us.

We are powerless against them.

They think that we are dead meat.

To them, it is not a matter of 'if' but of 'when.'

The vultures are circling.

"Do you think that there is an afterlife?" I was sitting on a rolling chair in Dad's hospital room. I knew that the end was at hand and was desperate to keep my connection with him for as long as possible.

"Nope. This is all that there is. That's the balance." He said softly. "Eternal life is not an afterlife. Permanence is eternal life. Nobody gives it to us, we need to earn it."

"I suppose the blighters who want to sell us all eternal salvation are going to be hacked off when they learn about that." I said with a grin.

"No more and no less than the people who study near death experiences will be. Wasting their time, that lot. They think that the brain's death spasms constitute a consciousness that is separate from the body. Bunch of wankers and snake oil salesmen. The people who 'die' and then come back... they experience the brain's equivalent of hypnic jerks.[31] The brain tries to survive, tries to jump-start itself and the body. But *nearly* dying is quite traumatic enough, especially if a person has a heart attack or some other injury that isn't instant death. The conscious mind realizes it's about to get a cosmic buggering. It panics. Creates all sorts of random cross-connections in major bursts across different brain centers, all in service of survival. It overwhelms the visual cortex, makes it think that there is a light to go toward and tosh like that."

"Did you pick that up from Klaatu?" I was curious as to whether or not this was his personal opinion, sans Klaatu's influence.

"Klaatu." His voice had a very Sir David Attenborough quality to it: sweetly serene, infinitely kind and wisened. "Nobody wants to die, unless they're defective. Never. Anyone. Anywhere. However, 'Life everlasting' has to be earned, obtained by the worthy, the evolved and enlightened. When you are dead, you are dead. When you are permanent, you are *permanent*."

---

[31] Hypnic jerks or myoclonic jerks are the phenomenon of an uncontrolled spasm. People most often experience them when they are falling asleep. The body spasms the person back to a waking state. Nobody knows for sure why this happens, but there are lots of SWAGs out there. GTS.

"So Klaatus don't die?" I asked, shocked.

"Only rarely, and only by accident, it would seem. Together, They form an eternal consciousness, with trillions of lives intertwined, all supporting each other, nurturing each other." He said, gently blinking his eyes and nodding his head.

As Dad lay dying, he told me that he believes that Klaatu does in-fact wants us to survive, despite all of our self-destructive shortcomings. He also said that he thought that Klaatu had very little expectation that we would save ourselves. When I asked him how he knew, and whether he had found something else in the report, he just held my hand and said that I'd have to take his word for it.

"So, you expect me to just take it on faith?" We both laughed out loud.

"I found a cipher in the report." He said, working hard to breathe as mesothelioma choked his lungs. "I just knew there had to be something hidden in there. I thought it was going to be less human-like, more sophisticated, like the two-hologram interference we talked about. I suppose that was just me being whimsical, a fanciful tit. Either that or Klaatu was slow pitching it to us dim-witted monkey boys. I so desperately wanted it to be a formulae for removing greenhouse gasses from the atmosphere or insights into the ways that other civilizations got past the pitfalls of money and religion... something... *anything* useful, practical.

"The clever sod based his cipher on pi, Euler's number, and the dimensions of the Great Pyramid of Cheops. It was quite an ingenious application of them, as one might expect. But then I suppose that cats find can openers ingenious, so there you have it." He laid his head back on his pillow and closed his eyes for a moment, gathering a teaspoon of strength. "That ought to make the crystal huggers and 'UFO researchers' double-down on their nonsense about aliens building the bloody pyramids." He wheezed with a weak chuckle.

"What was the message?" I asked, levitating above the edge of my seat.

He closed his eyes again and drew oxygen through the cannula in his nostrils, squeezing my hand for a long moment.

"Ozymandias[32]." He said, a tear rolling down his cheek.

There is the truth of it.

What are you going to do about it?

[32] It's back on page 4. If you didn't read it or you have forgotten it, now would be a great time to do so.

Afterword

After Dad passed away, as I was finalizing my thoughts on all of our conversations, I was struck suddenly by what Dad had once said to me: "Our entire reality is trapped inside of these three physical dimensions and they are inextricably linked to time *within those three physical dimensions*."

That, I believe, might be how the Klaatus can go from one end of the universe to the other in 'zero time': by getting out of at least one of our three physical dimensions. If They can pivot themselves so that They are outside of one or more of our three physical dimensions, They may no longer be "inextricably linked" to the time component of our space-time.

This of course will require that we be much more precise with how we employ the terminology of dimensions. Physicists refer to some things as being "one dimensional" even though they really are two or three. What they most frequently mean when they do this is that there is only one dimension of a phenomenon that they are interested in or are paying attention to in their research and that they intend to ignore the others, treating them as irrelevant. This is sheer sophistry.

If we could draw a one-dimensional line that is one meter long, it would have a length of one meter, a width of zero and a height of zero. That is not a line, that is an invisible, imaginary *concept*. There may be things that happen along that one-meter, but that does not mean that there is a line there. There might be an invisible, one dimensional thing there (like the field line of a magnet) but it is not a "thing" and it is probably two or three dimensional, having length and width and height.

"Things" in our reality have three dimensions associated with them, even if the measurements of those dimensions would be what scientists call "very, very small." There are no "one dimensional circuits." There are no zero-dimensional particles. When you hear about such things, do not think that it means anything other than that there is math involved that you do not understand and probably shouldn't.

Anyway, my mind has been mulling this over for a bit. If the Klaatu can move at a right angle to our space-time, say from X, Y, Z space into V, W, X space, they may be outside of our space-time, travel at near-light-speed, pivot back into X, Y, Z space and appear to have nearly instantaneously traversed a galaxy in zero time.

I do realize that this requires a huge number of assumptions, not the least of which is that there are V and W dimensions at right angles to our physical reality. There are good reasons to believe that this may be so, and there is some evidence that they do exist in the scientific literature.[33] Per one of the main points of this tale, our ignorance of such matters ought not to discourage our curiosity. Our assumptions about what we think that we know need to be recognized. If there are extra dimensions, we cannot assume that they are just like ours and that our physical laws work the same

---

33 Don't fall prey to the science priests' polemics. Remember how humans once thought that the earth was the center of the universe? "Look with your eyes!" Those "scientists" would yell. "You can *see* the planets and stars going around earth every night! There is no evidence that we are not at the center of creation." They were somewhat less than correct. Why? Sophomoric fallacy aside, they *assumed*, quite incorrectly, that they knew things that they did not (like the retrograde "orbits" of inner planets being ruled by ad hoc and nonsensical tosh). Most scientists today *think* that they *know* that other dimensions do not exist, even though they base their views on the *lack of evidence* for them, and make many assumptions that are unreasonable, unjustifiable and ignorant. "Stay scientific, Jerry."

way in them, nor that our 3D testing equipment will show us anything about 4D space. Why would we be walled off from them, as we clearly are, if everything worked the same way there that they do here? If they exist, it is because nature requires the isolation. That doesn't mean that we are not clever enough to fudge our way into it. This may also be the place where the physical mechanisms of quantum non-locality take place... There are really good reasons to look into the idea, is all that I suggest.

One thing is absolutely clear: we, our planet, galaxy and the visible universe exist in X, Y, Z space and no other dimension. Time is *not* a physical dimension, it is a *parameter*. It is a quantity that varies relative to other things within our X, Y, Z space. It is the measure of changes between things and nothing more.

I'm not here to debate the nose-pickers. Yes, we would have to assume that X, Y, Z stuff can actually exist in V, W, X space. We would have to further assume that there is a way to move through the V, W, X space, i.e. that it is not functionally a solid barrier to us for some reason, as if our three dimensions are a bubble trapped inside of concrete. That may actually explain why humans are not made of the right stuff for time work. We would also have to assume that Klaatus have an energy source that is powerful enough to allow them to travel into the other dimensions, or to travel at near light speed for extended periods, or both.[34] I say that because,

---

[34] Such a source does exist. If you have never heard of the zero-point field (ZPF), Google it. You will find that (1) it is real (2) it is a huge energy source and (3) scientists assume things about it that are not at all based on anything other than personal biases founded on ignorance and their 'expert say-so'. For example, they will tell us that all of the negative ZPF values must (a) cancel out all of the positive ones and (b) can't be isolated from the positive ones for use. That's as dumb as saying that batteries can't exist because all of the positive and negative electrical fields in the universe must cancel out to zero, and they can't be isolated. My flashlight begs to differ.

even though time will stand still for us, so to speak, Klaatus will probably have clocks running at normal speed in their craft. Or maybe not, I just do not know. But they are doing *something*, and we ought to try to figure it out.

There are many other things that would have to be true for this to be possible. But that is not the point.

The point is that it might behoove us to consider the possibilities rather than to arbitrarily reject them.

The point is, LISTEN TO THE LESSONS WE WERE GIVEN HEREIN AND KEEP AN OPEN MIND.

The point is, stop irrationally telling yourself that things can't be true because they make your brain uncomfortable. Remember how even Einstein fell into that trap and how he had to labor mightily to overcome his emotional misgivings in order to achieve legendary status.

Look for possibilities until there is solid, cogent proof that they cannot be true. If we as a species have one thing that we can be proud of, it is that our infinite curiosity, cleverness and potential renders very little impossible.

Our existence depends upon that kind of thinking.

R.R. 2024

About the Author

The author wishes to remain anonymous.

Please respect his or her wish.

I did ask nicely.

R.R.

Printed in Great Britain
by Amazon